STARTING RIGHT WITH

MILK GOATS

BY

HELEN WALSH

EDITED BY ED ROBINSON

British Library Cataloguing-in-Publication Data
A catalogue record for this book is available from the
British Library

Contents

19

Goat Farming

The domestic goat (*Capra aegagrus hircus*) is a subspecies of goat domesticated from the wild goat of southwest Asia and Eastern Europe. The goat is a member of the family Bovidae and there are now over 300 distinct breeds. Goats are one of the oldest domesticated species, and have been used for their milk, meat, hair, and skins over much of the world – their relationship with humans has an incredibly long, useful and varied history. The most recent genetic analysis confirms the archaeological evidence that the wild Bezoar ibex of the Zagros Mountains are the likely origin of almost all domestic goats today.

Neolithic farmers began to herd wild goats for easy access to milk and meat, primarily, as well as for their dung, which was used as fuel, and their bones, hair, and sinew for clothing, building, and tools. The earliest remnants of domesticated goats have been found in Iran, dating at around 10,000 years ago, and remains have also been found at archaeological sites in Jericho, Choga Mami Djeitun and Çayönü, dating the domestication of goats in Western Asia at between 8000 and 9000 years ago. Today (as then), Goat farming is a profitable business, due to its relatively low investments - and multi functional utility. A goat is useful to humans when it is living and when it is dead, first

1

as a renewable provider of milk, manure, and fibre, and then as meat and hide. Some charities even provide goats to impoverished people in poor countries, because goats are far easier and cheaper to manage than cattle – but provide just as much value.

The particular housing used for goats depends on the intended use of the animal, but also on the region of the world in which it is raised. Historically, domestic goats were generally kept in herds that wandered on hills or other grazing areas, often tended by goatherds who were frequently children or adolescents, similar to the more widely known shepherd; a method still used in the present day. Most commonly though, goats are kept for their dairy produce (especially in Asia and Nepal), which means they are far more likely to be kept in barns, close to the farm. Dairy goats are generally pastured in summer and may be stabled during the winter, whereas meat goats are more frequently pastured year-round, and may be kept many miles from their barns.

Aside from their uses for meat, dairy as well as their dung and hide, goats have been used by humans to clear unwanted vegetation for centuries. They have been described as 'eating machines' and 'biological control agents', and have proved incredibly successful in such endeavours. There has been a resurgence of this practice in North America since 1990, when herds were used to clear dry brush from California hillsides thought to be endangered by potential wildfires.

Since then, numerous public and private agencies have hired private herds to perform similar tasks. This practice has also become popular in the Pacific Northwest, where they are used to remove invasive species not easily removed by humans, including (thorned) blackberry vines and poison oak. This wonderful and diverse species continues to be of much use to the human race, and it is for this reason that goat farming retains its interest.

MISS HELEN WALSH OF GEORGETOWN, CONNECTI-
CUT, HAS BEEN A BREEDER OF GOATS FOR NEARLY
TWENTY YEARS.

STARTING RIGHT WITH MILK GOATS

Preface

I DON'T know why we Americans are so backward in our knowledge of goats or why so many of us simply say "NO"! to the idea of keeping goats when all we know about them is what we've read in the comic strips.

If you've never kept goats, never visited a modern goat dairy, never tasted carefully handled goat's milk—then by all means buy this book and learn some of the facts about the modern dairy goat. Milk and milk products account for 25 per cent of the average food budget—and a goat can efficiently turn the brush, weeds and hay in your back lot into good-tasting, naturally homogenized milk, cream, butter, cheese and ice cream.

For most twenty years Miss Helen Walsh, the author of this book, has been a leading breeder of milk goats. Probably she's helped as many beginners start in with goats as anyone else in this country.

She's good at explaining how to get started too. I know because five years ago I bought my first milk goat from her. During the following months I asked her advice many times— and it was always good!

Because of the dearth of material in book form on goat

keeping—and a greatly increased interest in the subject—I asked Miss Walsh if she'd write a complete manual for the beginner. She did, and here—after nearly three years' work—is the book.

You'll find "Starting Right With Milk Goats" complete, interestingly written, and wonderfully illustrated.

Ed Robinson

Author of "The 'Have-More' Plan"

1

There's Milk in Your Backyard

MISS EVA LEGALLIENNE, a neighbor of mine, once told me of a guest she had for luncheon on a hot summer day who asked for a glass of milk.

"Goat milk?" queried the maid.

"Oh, no!" the woman answered. "I couldn't drink goat milk—even if Miss LeGallienne does."

Miss LeGallienne and the maid exchanged understanding glances and soon a glass of cool milk was set before the guest. A person accustomed to goat milk would have recognized its whiteness, but the inexperienced guest drank the milk and remarked, "My, that was delicious!"

"We never told her," said Miss LeGallienne, "and to this day she doesn't know she enjoyed a glass of goat milk."

I have had a number of such experiences. A woman wanted milk for her husband who had stomach ulcers. She was quite sure that he wouldn't drink it if he knew that he was getting goat milk, so she changed the cap on the bottle.

She worried when her husband tasted the milk and

immediately demanded, "Where did you get *this* milk?"

"Oh, from a nearby dairy," his wife answered. "Why?"

"It's the best milk I ever tasted . . ." her husband replied.

It was a long time before she dared tell him he was drinking goat milk. But when she did he was so sold on it that he had no prejudice left.

I guess everybody who has kept goats has had some sort of similar experience. Ed Robinson, author of "The 'Have-More' Plan," tells about the time he was asked to give a luncheon talk before the Bridgeport Lion's Club. Even though it was in the main dining-room of the swank Stratfield Hotel, he brought along one of his goats, milked her, and had over fifty people compare goat and cow milk. About one-third said the goat milk was cow milk, another third said the cow milk was goat milk, and, of course, the rest guessed correctly.

Properly handled goat milk is almost impossible to distinguish from cow milk by tasting. Most of the prejudice against goat milk seems to come from people who have had it abroad where a picturesque herdsman milked it into a bowl. Perhaps his hands and the goat's udder were clean, but more likely they weren't. You know enough about milk and butter to know that even in your own refrigerator they absorb odors quickly. Also, some people in this country who have goats make the mistake of letting the male run with their milking goats. A buck, at certain times, *does* smell—and this odor is often picked up by the milkers. Moreover, goat milk, like cow milk, *must* be chilled immediately after milking—but more about this later on.

I have kept goats for many years—about fifteen to be exact. Obviously, I like them. But in this book I want to write about them objectively. I want to talk about all their good points—and their bad points too. For goatkeeping, like most everything else I know of, has its disadvantages.

First, let us consider the happy side of goatkeeping.

Milk and milk products account for 25 per cent of the average family's food budget. A goat is an extremely efficient small milk producer. A good goat should average two to three quarts of milk per day for ten months; the latter two months she should be rested before she has her young and, of course, begins another ten months' cycle of milk production. If two goats are kept you can have one milking at all times. Even if you buy all the grain a goat eats it costs 10 cents or less a day to feed a milking goat; the sale of her annual kid or kids should pay for incidental expenses such as veterinarian fees, breeding fees, etc.

This little girl finds Saanen kids excellent playmates.

Goat milk is good milk. Today, some 60 per cent of the milk consumed throughout the world is goat milk. It is easier than cow milk to digest; it is naturally homogenized. That is, the fat globules, which are smaller than those in cow milk, stay in suspension. Many people, particularly infants, who cannot digest cow milk thrive on goat milk. A survey of people owning goats would probably show that a large percentage purchased their first doe because of some illness or allergy in the family, for from the days of Hippocrates, the father of medicine, down to the present, goat milk has been advised by physicians in the treatment of many human ailments.

A goat does not need as large nor as expensive quarters as a cow. Many people, particularly women who feel that a cow is too much to handle, can and do keep goats. Goats thrive on woodsy pasture; brush, weeds and poison ivy are manna from heaven.

Many families believe that they can use only two to four quarts of milk a day. Two goats should keep them supplied, whereas a cow that gives ten to twenty quarts a day would swamp them.

A goat is only a sixth the size of a cow and therefore can be transported to a veterinarian, or to a buck in the family car. Goats average from 166 to 202 births per hundred, depending on the breed; that is, your goat is more apt to have two kids than one . . . three kids are not uncommon and occasionally even four. A goat has a somewhat longer productive life than a cow. Goat milk sold retail brings a high price—25 to 60 cents a quart. It takes less capital to buy a couple of goats than a cow. Goat meat, called chevon, is good to eat and hard to distinguish from lamb.

Goats are friendly, intelligent, and responsive to human affection. The young goats are capricious, fun to watch, and make excellent pets for children.

An idyllic street scene at Saanen in the Bernese Oberland, Switzerland. The goats shown in this picture are, of course, of the noted Saanen breed.

Now for some disadvantages. If you are going to keep goats, or any animal that has to be milked, somebody must be at home to milk twice a day. Milking should be done regularly. Goats are perhaps the most difficult of all livestock to keep fenced; they will jump or climb any fence less than 48 inches high. If they are not properly fenced they will get out and you can count on them browsing on your choicest young apple trees or shrubbery. It is as much trouble to make TB and Bang's tests on a single goat as it is on a cow. Because goats can be bred usually only in the fall and winter months it is more difficult to plan steady, year-round milk production. Even though goat milk brings more than cow milk, customers are more scattered and more expensive to locate. Generally, goat keepers do not keep records of production and it is harder to buy a good goat than it is to buy a good cow.

The little boy who lives next door makes friends with some of my Nubian kids.

How many people believe the disadvantages are outweighed by the advantages? For the first time, the census in 1940 covered milk goats—and found 118,896 were "milked during any part of 1939 on 33,232 farms." The census goes on to say that "since 876,596 goats were enumerated that were not classified as Angoras (which are kept for mohair) and only 118,896 were reported milked in 1939, it is apparent that there is still a large population of goats classified as 'brush goats.' Their chief utility seems to be the clearing up of brush pastures, wood lots, and rough land, but they also contribute to the supply of kid and goat meat in southern and southwestern states. The number of goats milked covered only 3.6 per farm reporting. However, in some areas there were producing flocks of considerable size. Some of these larger flocks were adjacent to large city markets, but the largest ones were in the Southwest where much of the milk was used for manufacture of cheese."

Since over 100,000 people in this country see good reason for keeping milk goats—there must be something in it.

2

What Breed to Buy?

DON'T rush off now and buy the first goat you see, much as you would buy a bag of salt. Take it easy, and first learn something about goats.

By the way, learn that the proper term for a female goat is doe, for a male, buck, and if you would have the goodwill of goat lovers don't refer to them as nanny goats and billy goats. Goat people hate this just as you would hate hearing your children called brats.

Noah was a good man, and he was also a wise man. When he equipped the Ark he put into it two animals of each species. His primary purpose, of course, was propagation, but he also knew that no animal can be happy alone. You will find that your goat will be happier with a companion and will make fewer demands on your attention. You might buy two milkers, if you need that amount of milk, or you might get a milker and a yearling—a debutante, so to speak—one just reaching maturity. Goats are seasonal milkers, milking usually for eight or ten months. By breeding the yearling so that she will have a baby kid and begin to give milk—which is called freshening—before the milker goes dry you can keep a supply of milk throughout the year. Or you might buy a milker and a kid. But be sure it is a doe kid.

After you have held a family council and decided that you want goats, visit the goat breeders in your section of the country, look over their stock and talk goats with them. Most goat raisers love their animals and love to talk about them and, generally speaking, will give you freely of their knowledge. It is preferable to buy your goats from such a source, for these people know how to feed and care for the goats, their animals have been tested for TB and Bang's disease, just as cows are tested, and you will know that the milk is safe for use.

You will find, as you go about, that each breeder specializes in raising one or more types of goats, and that there are four popular breeds. These breeds are Toggenburg, Saanen, Nubian, and Alpine.

Toggenburgs, originating in Switzerland, are almost uniformly some shade of brown, with a white stripe at either side of the face from eye to muzzle, a white area around the tail and white hocks. There are, however, occasional variations toward grey coloring, or even spots of white on the coat infrequently. Their faces are slightly concave between the eyes—"dished" they are called—their ears are prick or stand-up, their coats either short or long haired (usually long haired in the buck), and does as well as bucks have beards.

Saanens, also from Switzerland, are large, white or cream white animals with dished faces and prick ears, and are either short or long haired. Occasionally a Saanen will show spots of grey or touches of black, but the goal of the Saanen breeders is the pure white animal. The Saanen doe also is bearded.

Anglo-Nubians, commonly referred to as Nubians, may easily be recognized by their large, drooping ears and humped (Roman) noses. They were originated by the British by crossing the native goat with bucks from Africa. They are always short haired, but of no specific color. They may be of various shades of brown, black, white, cream, buff, grey or combinations of these colors.

French Alpines are large animals with cone-shaped ears and slightly concave faces. They too may be white, black, brown, grey or combinations of these colors. In the cou blanc type the front part of the body is light in color, shading into black hind quarters. Chamoisees are brown with black on head, legs and back; sundgaus black with white on face and under-part of body. Their hair is sleek and short.

Famous bucks and does who helped establish their breeds here and from whom many present day goats are descended.

Upper. Prince Bismarck from Switzerland and Polly Mac. (Toggenburgs). *Lower.* Lunesdale Spurius Lartius from England and Shirley Rona, his daughter, from Canada. (Nubians)

Rock Alpines, similar in appearance to the French Alpines, were originated in this country by Mrs. Mary Rock, who crossed the French Alpine with Toggenburg and Saanen stock. The Rock Alpine is the only breed of American origin.

A purebred is an animal of unmixed breed, descended from stock that traces entirely within the blood lines of the foundation stock of the breed. A grade is an animal one of whose parents is a purebred and the other a scrub or an animal containing a considerable proportion of the blood of the same breed as the purebred parent. If the dam is purebred the offspring derives her breed classification from either parent. A doe resulting from the breeding of a registered buck with a

20

doe not purebred takes her breed classification from that of the sire. For example, a doe kid born to a doe of mixed breed bred to a registered Toggenburg buck would be 1/2 Toggenburg; the next generation would be 3/4 Toggenburg; then 7/8 and so on. This method of breeding each generation to a registered sire of the same breed is known as "grading up" and results in a fairly rapid improvement of stock.

There are two associations for the registration of goats, established to promote and improve the dairy goat industry in this country. The American Goat Society registers only purebreds. The American Milk Goat Record Association registers purebreds and also records as grades does or doe kids that are up to 15/16 of a particular breed. When the 31/32 generation is reached the animal may be registered in this association as "American" of the breed, such as American Toggenburg, American Nubian, etc.

Membership in these associations costs a small fee and yearly dues, and both associations register animals of non-members as well as of members.

If you purchase a purebred goat be sure that you secure her registration papers at the time of sale. Sometimes the inexperienced buyer fails to do this and finds later (as I did) that the seller "can't find the papers," and the socalled purebred can't be registered, nor can her kids, except as grades. Here, again, your protection lies in buying from a reliable breeder, for he has a reputation to maintain and his statements can usually be depended on.

Don't, however, be swept off your feet at the mere thought of papers with your animal, for unless the papers cover a good animal from productive ancestors their chief value is historic. Any breeder with a registered animal to sell will give you a transcript of its genealogy and tell you something of its history. Also there is much valuable information on individual animals and blood lines to be found in the trade publications—*American Goat News, Dairy Goat Journal, Better Goatkeeping* and *The Goat World*—and in the writings of various goat breeders who have contributed articles to these magazines. Mr. J. S. Fetter of Coldwater, Ohio, for example, has written exhaustively on the subject of Saanens and Saanen importations. Mr. E. S. Thompson of Bristol, Pa., and Mrs. Evelyn Latourette, Estacado, Oregon, have covered Toggenburgs, and for information on these two Swiss breeds there is the Swiss Goat Club of which Mrs. Latourette is secretary. On Nubians Mrs. Carl Sandburg of Flat Rock, North Carolina, and Mr. Lyle Hulbert of Rome, New York, have contributed largely of their knowledge and on French Alpines there are the writings of Mrs. F. N. Craver of El Paso, Texas. On Rock Alpines there are the records of Mrs. Mary Rock, the founder of the breed.

A few more bucks and does.

Upper. Panama Louise from Switzerland and Panama Prince Fribourg. (Saanen) *Lower.* Le Poilu and Molly Crepin—two of the several bucks and does used to develop the Rock Alpine breed.

Even if you are purchasing a grade goat you can learn much about its heredity by investigating the history of its sire.

The following data on breed production is interesting.

23

However, be sure to bear in mind that there is great individual variation in animals.

The 1945 Advanced Registry reports, as summarized in March 1946 *Better Goatkeeping*, show:

The average tested French Alpine gave 1985.3 lbs. of 3.7% milk.

The average tested Nubian gave 1626.5 lbs of 5.02% milk.

The average tested Rock Alpine gave 1950.0 lbs. of 4% milk.

The average tested Saanan gave 2325.9 lbs. of 3.59% milk.

The average tested Toggenburg gave 1902.3 lbs. of 3.18% milk.

3

How to Buy a Good Doe

WHEN you go to look at a goat, notice the general appearance of the animal. Is she alert, clear eyed, her coat shiny? If the answer is "yes" it should be an indication of good health. Steer clear of the goat who is "nice and fat," for while a dairy goat should not be thin and gaunt, she should not be of the chunky, beef-cattle type.

Notice the general formation of her body-conformation. See that her hind legs are spaced apart sufficiently to allow for development of a good-sized udder, which should be firmly attached, not sagging, with teats that can be easily grasped. Milking a goat can be a pleasure, but it is far from it if she has a generous udder with small teats. See that the animal has a well rounded "barrel" which shows capacity for digesting quantities of bulky food such as hay. If you can be on hand when she is milked notice if her udder shows an appreciable shrinkage in size after she has been milked. It should; otherwise you may suspect that the good-sized udder isn't well filled with milk, but consists mostly of muscular tissue.

If you are buying a yearling or a kid and her mother and sire are present, look them over so that you may know what to expect when the youngster matures. In my very early days I was on the point of buying a young doe because she had blue eyes—the only time I had seen a blue-eyed goat. Then I saw the mother who, although purebred, was very small and had been bred prematurely. Common sense told me that much shouldn't be expected of the kid and although it was hard to resist the blue eyes I reluctantly let common sense rule the day.

If the person from whom you purchase operates a dairy, you will undoubtedly find that his goats have been tested for tuberculosis and Bang's disease, or brucillosis. If they have not been tested, it is well to have these tests made, for, although neither disease is often found in goats, your source of raw milk needs to be above question as to its wholesomeness.

What should you pay for a goat? Prices vary in different sections of the country and at different seasons of the year. Because the large percentage of goats freshen during the late winter and early spring, winter milkers are not easy to obtain, and a doe giving milk during the winter months, if she can be purchased, will bring a price somewhat higher than she might at other seasons when more milkers are available. You will find, however, that a fairly uniform price will prevail in your section which may vary from $25 to $75 for grades, $40 to several hundred for purebreds.

How much milk should you expect from your doe? According to the U. S. Department of Agriculture, a goat giving 2 quarts a day is a good milker, one giving 3 quarts excellent. For advanced registry tests a two-year-old doe (which means a doe on her first freshening) is required to show an average milk production of approximately 2 1/2 quarts a day over a period of 10 months. This is a sort of roll of honor registry and means that the goat who earns her letters AR is better than average. Because you are accustomed to think of milk in quarts, as you buy it, I am giving the figures in approximate quarts, but actually the milk is weighed—a pint equalling approximately a pound. And the requirement is 1500 pounds of milk or 52 pounds of butterfat over a test period of 305 days, allowing 60 days' rest period before kidding without test, during which time the doe normally should be dry. If these letters AR appear on the registration certificates of your doe's parents and grandparents it is reasonable to assume that she herself has promise of being a good milker.

Daily Production and Fat Content of Goat's Milk

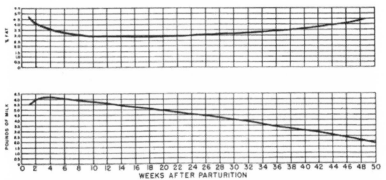

WEEKS AFTER PARTURITION

EFFECT OF PERIOD OF LACTATION ON THE DAILY PRODUCTION OF MILK AS RE-
PRESENTED BY COMPOSITE SAMPLES OF THE MILK OF SAANENS AND TOGGENBURGS

Maximum milk production ordinarily increases after each fresh-ening until the fifth to eighth year when a doe is at her peak.

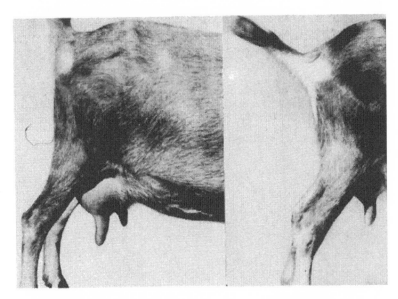

Left. Goat's udder before milking. Right. Udder after milking.

Your neighbor may tell you of someone she knew whose goat gave six or seven quarts. Perhaps so, but people are funny about goats. Sometimes they tell tall stories, like the fisherman with his big catch. Six- and seven-quart milkers can be found, but not usually in a home dairy.

In purchasing a milking doe you may arrange to see her milked and know just what she is producing. If she is not milking you will have to trust to the integrity of the seller and judge from her past record or her breeding what she is likely to produce. Don't be disturbed and assume that you have been duped if, after you take her home, she drops in production. Goats are very sensitive to changes in environment, handling and feeding, and show it immediately in a lessened milk output. After she becomes accustomed to you, and to her new home, she will give more milk, although it sometimes takes weeks before a doe is back to maximum production. Don't assume either that the doe will keep up a steady output for the entire period of lactation. She has a high peak, usually two or three months after kidding, and a low ebb as she nears the end of her lactation period. The figures above are averaged.

Four does from one herd that won the Governor's Trophy for Best Eight Head, Toggenburg breed. Notice the breed characteristics: white strips from head to muzzle . . . white around tail and hocks.

4

The Goat's Quarters

THERE is nothing that leads to trouble quicker than getting a goat before you have a barn and pasture ready. Inevitably, your goat will get loose and eat up your most valuable shrubbery—or become so messy in temporary, hard-to-clean quarters that you will wish you had never heard of goats.

This doesn't mean that you must build a new and elaborate barn, In fact, the reverse is true—almost any small barn, shed or poultry house can be remodeled into satisfactory goat quarters. Just get everything ready before you bring home your doe.

The thing to bear in mind is that you want your layout of the goat barn to be as efficient and time-saving as possible. Makeshift arrangements are terribly expensive in the amount of time and energy they waste. Each minute you can cut off chore time means a saving of twelve hours a year!

What are satisfactory quarters for goats? First, the quarters should not be located too far from the house. Goats, or almost any livestock, do better if they are fed three light meals a day instead of just a heavy morning and night feeding. Also a trip to the barn at noontime, just to "look in" at your animals, is a good idea. Your barn ought not to be so far away that a long wade through snowdrifts is necessary.

Now, about the barn itself. It should be free of drafts. Goats can stand considerable cold—but not drafts. Also see that roof and walls are rainproof. The barn should preferably face south or southeast. A door should lead directly out of the barn into the fenced pasture. Stalls should be arranged for easy feeding and cleaning. Provision should be made for sanitary manure disposal. Running water via a frost-proof hydrant will very nearly cut chore time in half. Grain should be protected from rats. Covered galvanized waste barrels make good grain containers. Space for hay storage must be provided. Either the barn should be constructed with an inside corral or a shelter should be provided in the pasture so that your goats can take cover from summer rain squalls or winter winds. You should have a milk stand to make milking easy. An outdoor hay rack is a good idea too. A low ceiling (6 1/2 or 7 feet), particularly in northern United States, helps to retain the natural heat of your animals. While a goat can stand zero weather, the energy the animal expends in keeping warm might better be spent in making milk.

Upper. Home-made tie-stalls for four milkers. Notice dairy gutter in cement floor . . . also first two stalls show removable floors; the rear portion is slatted to keep milkers clean. Lower left. A small goat dairy barn. Lower right. Goat stalls with stanchions. The fittings for this type of goat stall may be purchased ready-made.

For a few goats, stalls that will permit them to move about—box-stalls—are preferable to tie-stalls, for goats are naturally very active animals. The box-stalls are not so easily cleaned as the tie-stalls, however. The box-stall should be at least 3 × 5 feet with a manger for grain and hay feeding. Feeding grain in a pan on the floor means waste, grain spilled and soiled with manure so that the goat won't eat it.

If the floor of the stall is of cement it should drain, and have a wooden-slatted platform or a heavy wire-mesh platform that can be removed and cleaned. In the box-stall the floor should have a covering of straw, peat moss, waste hay or leaves to prevent trouble developing in the goat's udder from lying in the cold and wet. Each goat should have her own stall which should be provided with a salt container holding a block of iodized salt, a deep pan rather than a pail for drinking water (the handle of the pail is apt to catch over the goat's head with disastrous results).

For companionship it is well to have the stalls side by side with the dividing partition high enough so that the goats cannot climb over, and strong enough to resist the butting contests that even goats that are good friends will occasionally indulge in. Have the gates open inward. It is more convenient for you when you enter with an armful of hay and resists better any attempt of the goat to open the gate herself. If you use slatted gates, don't let the slats stick up like pickets on a fence with the chance that a young kid will get caught between the slats or an older goat catch her hoof between them, and have the cross braces on the outside to prevent a goat climbing on them with undue strain on the hinges.

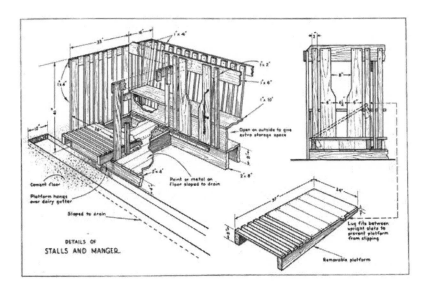

DETAILS OF
STALLS AND MANGER

Try to have your "milk-room" arranged in a separate section at least large enough to hold your milking bench if space is limited, so that the goat may be taken from her stall for milking. It is far more sanitary than milking her in her stall, or nearby. You will also need to provide some space for grain and hay where it will be convenient for you to get at it, but out of the goat's reach. In so far as it is possible, equip your goat shed with a view to making the work as simple and easily handled as possible. Makeshifts try your patience and make a hard job out of an easy one. Have a special place for brooms, shovels, pitchforks, rakes, etc., to avoid accident to yourself and to the goats, and keep them there. If you haven't space for a closet, a wooden bar, much like a towel rack, can be nailed against the wall and the utensils for cleaning held behind it.

A commercial barn for the goats presupposes that you intend to have considerably more than two. In this event you will need two or three box-stalls for kidding, but may prefer tie-stalls for stanchioning the goats which makes the cleaning less work, and gives the barn a neat, trim appearance.

You will also need space for the storage of hay. A mow conserves floor space but is not nearly as practical as storage on the main floor. The opening of the mow through which the hay is dropped should be so placed that the hay doesn't fall onto the floor between the gutters where it will become soiled with manure and unusable. Have a small room for grain, a room at least 8 × 10 feet in which to keep your milking bench and do the milking, and a third small room in which the milk may be bottled, with space for a sink, a refrigerator and racks for milking equipment. Such an arrangement gives you the basis for a commercial dairy if you plan to sell milk.

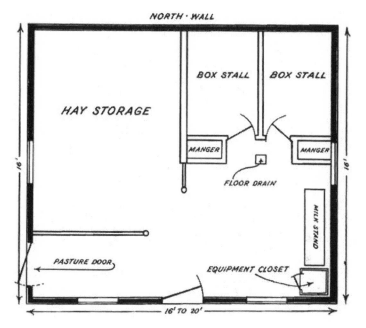

Two-Goat Barn.

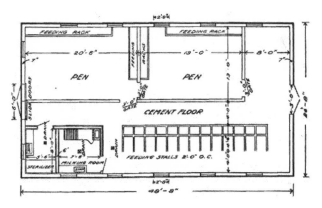

Commercial Goat Barn.

37

In the barn proper arrange a small closet in which to keep shovels, brooms, etc., with a shelf for disinfectants, pans and other incidental equipment.

It is also advisable to have at one end of the barn an area blocked off for an exercise pen. Here on stormy days the goats can have their fun while the stalls are being put in order. My exercise pen, a small one, is partitioned off with a length of fence wire so that the goats can see what is going on and enjoy a little exercise period even on the stormiest days. It opens into the field and on hot summer days or during a sudden shower is a haven for comfort and protection.

5

Feeding for More Milk

BEFORE the goats arrive have their feed on hand. Otherwise you will find yourself in the predicament of Old Mother Hubbard with a bare larder and hungry animals, for goat food can't be had at the corner grocery store. Some people have the idea that a goat can be staked out to eat up the green stuff on the place and everything will be lovely with a full milk pail at the end of the day. This is a long way from the fact. Goats left to forage entirely for their food are brush goats and are not expected to produce milk.

To make milk, dairy goats need grain and hay winter, summer and all the year. When pasture is good they will eat very little hay, but before starting out in the morning should be given a light feeding to sustain them until the dew has dried from the growing things. This breakfast of hay will also minimize the danger of their eating poisonous plants in the pasture which might attract them if they are very hungry. On stormy days when they must remain indoors—for goats dislike rain and wet weather—they need hay, and during the night they will nibble on hay with relish and benefit.

The leguminous hays—alfalfa, clover—are the best milk

producers and also the most expensive to buy. If you can afford to set your goats' table with alfalfa they will pay you dividends in increased milk production and sleek, shining coats and healthy bodies. However, a goat will eat and thrive on almost any sweet smelling, properly cured hay provided it is not stalky. If there are bits of brush and leaves mixed in she will relish it even more.

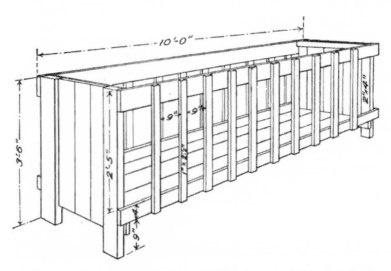

Combination hay and grain rack with bottom for feeding both roughage and grain.

During the season when pasture is scant a goat needs at least three pounds of hay daily, but the safe procedure is to allow her all the hay she will eat—not in one daily feeding, but at intervals—three or four feedings during the day, not too much at a time. In this way she will waste less. A goat is much like a child and will pick out the choice bits first, scattering the less desirable pieces in her efforts to find what she likes best. She has a reputation of being very wasteful of her hay, but with the kind she likes, fed in moderate amounts and placed in a properly constructed rack she does a pretty good job of cleanly eating it. Any that she tosses to the floor can be gathered up, if the floor is clean, and placed in a rack outside in her yard to be picked over again at her leisure and the residue set aside for bedding.

Goats are very active animals and need as much freedom as you can possibly allow them. If you have sufficient space, the happiest arrangement for your animals is a fenced-in pasture. This permits them to roam about selecting the growing things that appeal to their appetite, gives them needed exercise and opportunity to find a shady spot when the day is hot, and protects them from dogs.

It is well, however, before the goats are given freedom of the pasture, to make a careful inspection for poisonous plants. The number of these to be found throughout the country runs into the hundreds, but they are not all found in the same locality. There are certain species rather widely distributed among which are the various types of laurel and these you should learn to recognize, for they are deadly poisonous—sometimes in very small amounts (I have known of a goat dying after eating a little of a discarded Christmas wreath). Wild cherry also is widely scattered and the early shoots which young stock is apt to eat, and the leaves in their wilted state will produce prussic acid poisoning, frequently with fatal results. Goats can eat the more mature leaves and the dried wild cherry as well as the bark with apparently no ill effects. Roots of the water hemlock are most deadly to all animals, but since goats do not burrow for their food, danger to them from this plant is less frequently met. Common bracken, of the fern family, is another plant to be avoided. Loco weed is a very dangerous plant of which there are many varieties and oddly enough it is of the same botanical family as the much desired alfalfa.

These plants are not generally found in open pastures, but in the wooded and swampy sections. Your state department of agriculture will give you information about the poisonous plants native to your particular locality and it is your job to clear them out if they are present in your pasture.

The usual signs of forage poisoning are vomiting, frothing, staggering and convulsions with cries of pain and erratic leaping about. Sometimes, if the attack is not severe a teaspoonful of bicarbonate of soda placed dry into the animal's mouth will increase the vomiting and help to throw off the poisonous cud, or epsom salts as a drench will purge it from the system. Syringes for administering liquids may be obtained from veterinary supply houses, and it is well to have one on hand, but in emergency a tonic or similar bottle may be used.

Five Poisonous Plants

Upper left. Brake fern. *Upper right.* Loco weed, *Aragallus lambertii. Center.* Mountain laurel. *Lower left.* European Hemlock. *Lower right.* Wild cherry.

Drenching a goat, however, is a very serious undertaking and should not be resorted to unless no veterinarian is available. Under no circumstances should a novice or nervous person try it. If it must be done, get the animal onto her feet and put one leg on either side of her body holding her with pressure of your knees. It may be necessary to tie her. Insert the neck of the bottle or syringe at the side of her mouth, but don't press down on her tongue. She must have free movement of her tongue in order to swallow. Don't raise her head above a horizontal position and be very careful to pour the liquid slowly and gradually in very small amounts. If she struggles, stop. It's better to spill the liquid than to get it into her lungs, for that will mean her death. Follow the treatment with warm goat milk or black coffee, using the same care in administering it. Be gentle and talk to her so that she will not be frightened. In treating a very sick animal or a kid to whom you hesitate to give a drench, a wad of absorbent cotton soaked in the liquid and pressed between the goat's teeth at the side of the mouth, although a slow process, is effective.

If it is necessary to tether your goats, use a chain or hemp rope, not too heavy, with a swivel at either end to prevent tangling. Never use cotton, clothesline rope. Change their grazing place each day (they will not eat on ground that has been soiled with droppings) and place water within reach. Check on them occasionally to be sure that they are safe and comfortable and are finding sufficient green food to keep them contented.

In any case have at least a small, fenced exercise yard just outside their quarters so arranged that they can go inside for shelter from storm or sun. The yard is best on the south side so that it can be used even in winter when it would be impossible to tether them out-of-doors. This little yard will save you much anxiety, but it is an exercise yard solely and not meant for grazing.

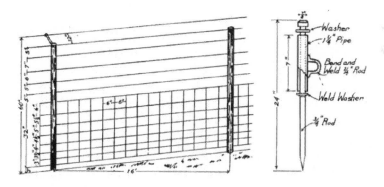

A post and wire fence for goats and a non-tangle tethering stake almost any garage man can easily make.

If you value your goats don't tether them out and go off for the day. You are apt to return and find that a goat has been attacked by dogs or has tangled in her chain and strangled. These two accidents are the most frequently reported disasters that happen to goats. In this connection it is not advisable to encourage a too friendly relationship between your dog and the goats. Goats and dogs can and do get along amicably, and work dogs are used on the ranges for herding sheep and goats, but with the household dog living in close, intimate contact with the household goat, there is always the danger that an incident will arise when the goat will butt the dog who will retaliate in a dog's language, and even a powerful buck is not equipped by nature for prolonged battle with an angry dog. My own dog, brought up with the goats from puppy days, helped to kill a goat whom apparently she loved above all the rest, and from various goat owners I have known many cases of goats killed or badly torn by dogs.

A four- or five-foot cattle wire fence makes a very substantial enclosure and protection for goats, or a two-wire electric fence is used by many people with success, but in no case should barbed wire be used. With a high fence it is not needed, and a low fence topped with barbed wire will not restrain a goat nor keep out a dog, but will mean instead ears or udder torn by the wire. If you cannot have a fenced-in pasture and must tether the goats, whenever possible take them with you on a trip through the woods. They will follow along as happily as a dog and stay closer by your side. Or while you are working out-of-doors let them wander about, but watch out that they don't nip off your choicest roses. If you fear for your trees, for as the season wanes some goats will nibble at the bark, smear the trunks now and then with a broom dipped in manure and they will keep away.

On days when the goats cannot be staked out it is well to cut green feed or to supply them with succulent feed such as beet pulp soaked in water, or vegetables—carrots, turnips, cabbage—almost any kind of vegetable except onions which they don't like. A general rule as to quantity to feed is 6 pounds per 100 pounds of body weight. An average doe might be fed 4 pounds of green stuff twice a day. This will keep up their milk production.

In fact, it is a good plan to plant a few rows of root vegetables and cabbage in the kitchen garden just for the goats. The English goatkeepers go in strongly for kale which is hardy and grows late into the fall. At all times cuttings from vegetables and fruit are good goat food and help to produce milk. If you add such food as a new part of a goat's diet, you will very likely see a definite increase in milk production. Such succulent food should form part of the goat's diet especially when pasture is limited or the grazing season ended.

Grain is a concentrated food and should be fed with caution. Too heavy grain feeding may result in indigestion or overproduction of milk with ultimate burning out of the goat's ability to produce any milk at all.

In the early days of goatkeeping, the goat owner had to mix his own feeds—a somewhat hit or miss procedure even when a specific formula is followed. There is no way the layman knows for determining how much actual food value there may be in a given bag of oats or corn. And mixing your own feed is a real chore. Your spirits droop when you see it getting low in the barrel. Nowadays, the various grain companies prepare grain combinations especially intended for goats, feeds which contain all the essential components, including minerals, which perhaps the individual might find unobtainable. For example, people living in New England, Delaware, Pennsylvania, and the Eastern Shore of Maryland can obtain a sheep and goat feed manufactured by the Eastern States Farmers Exchange (a cooperative association) which goats will eat day after day with relish. The formula for this food, developed after actual experiments with goats, lists yellow corn, crimped oats, bran, linseed and soybean meal, corn gluten meal, molasses, iodized salt, irradiated yeast, calcium carbonate, dicalcium phosphate (found in milk). Now what individual can attempt to assemble an assortment such as this for his goats? Yet these ingredients are, in the judgment of competent people, essential in a balanced diet.

Wherever you live, you will probably find that the local grain company carries a feed prepared specifically for goats and unless you raise your own grain in properly fertilized soil it is easiest and safest to rely on the product of the grain dealer. Dairy rations may be had in finely ground form, but most goats prefer the coarser mixtures or the pellets—something that they can crunch.

The amount of grain fed depends on the needs of the individual animal.

For milkers it is determined by the milk production, the ratio being 1 pound of grain with a protein content of 16 per cent for each 3 pounds of milk (approximately 3 pints) the goat produces.

For pregnant does: In the diet of pregnant does, the grain feeding should be lessened with their lessening milk production, and during the last two months of pregnancy when the doe should be dry it should not exceed 1 to 1 1/2 pounds daily. To this may be added bran for bulk and laxative quality.

For dry stock the allowance is 1 pound daily which may be increased if the animal is thin and in need of additional food.

For bucks 1 to 2 pounds daily is adequate, depending on the size of the animal and the service required of him.

For kids: Kids should be offered grain at one to two weeks old—a fine mixture such as a calf starter at first—and at about a month old they too can be given the coarser grain mixture fed to the older goats, as much as they will eat up at a feeding.

Grain should be given in two feedings, usually before milking. The doe is then contented and quiet while being milked. But whether you feed before or after milking be consistent in the method you use and always clear away any remnants of feed or hay in the racks before putting in the new meal. Sometimes people have complained that their goats don't eat up their grain, and on inquiry I have found that the fresh supply is put in on top of the leftover. Goats like a clean table to eat from just as humans do. Perhaps the goat has rested her hoof on the edge of the feed box opening and manure has dropped in—not enough to be apparent except to her sensitive nose—and in this event she will refuse her grain no matter how hungry she may be.

Some people fix a container on the milking bench and feed the goat while she is being milked. I tried this method when I had only a few goats, but it meant waiting until the doe finished her grain even though the milking was completed, or forcing her to leave the unfinished dish reluctantly. Also I found that some goats objected to eating from another's pan—one doe would not eat her grain unless a clean paper was spread on the shelf! Fed in their own stalls, they finish their grain down to the last speck and none is wasted.

If a goat goes "off her feed" as occasionally they do, a meal of bran or stale bread cut into small pieces will usually restore her appetite, or plain oats or some delicacy such as corn flakes.

Experiment with her yourself until you find the thing that appeals. Sometimes putting such a goat beside a good eater will stimulate her appetite—the dog-in-the-manger idea.

When grain is bought in small quantities, metal barrels are ideal for storing grain so rats can't get into it.

Fed a properly balanced grain mixture supplemental feeding of minerals should not be necessary, particularly if alfalfa hay forms a part of the diet. But salt, preferably iodized salt which may be obtained in brick form from your grain dealer, should always be accessible.

SILAGE FOR YOUR GOATS

Much as you will love your goats there are parts of the grounds where they can't be allowed to wander at will without damage to shrubs and trees and to the garden. These are the places where your lawn mower and sickle get into action to keep weeds and grass under control. If the goats are getting plenty of pasture these cuttings won't interest them much, if at all, even though they would like the chance to make a raid on them on their own. Yet if a spell of dry weather comes, or several rainy days that mean housing in the barn with dry roughage, these very clippings would be accepted readily. If you are handy, a small silo may be constructed into which the clippings may be stored to be fed out at just such times. Any forage that the animals like to eat green will make suitable silage, just take care that no wild cherry, which sometimes sends out new shoots close to the ground, laurel or rhododendron leaves, or other poisonous plants are included in your cuttings.

There are a few fundamentals to be kept in mind in

the making of such silage. It is most important that air be excluded and to this end the sides of the silo must be made airtight and the material packed in tightly, either by tramping it down if the silo is large enough or tamping it and placing a weight on top, being sure that it is distributed evenly so that no air spaces are left at the sides, for the presence of air causes oxidation and the silaged material will get moldy and unfit for use. The clippings are best chopped into 1/4-inch lengths and in wilted condition when placed in the silo. Technically, the proper moisture content when put in is 68 per cent— not wetter, and not drier than 58 per cent. The rapidity with which the cuttings will dry on the ground depends, of course, on the size of the swaths, the amount of sunlight they get, the humidity of the air, and the wind. If they are too dry when added, packing is difficult and some of the valuable carotene is lost, and if too wet much of the juice will leak out, be smelly and attract flies, and eventually rot the silo. Also, moist clippings make less palatable silage with less food value. If the material seems too wet and it isn't advisable to leave it longer on the ground because of the possibility of rain or because of other duties, finely chopped, good quality hay may be added which will soak up some of the moisture.

Left. An ordinary 10-cent scrub brush makes a good brush for goats. The people are Ed and Carolyn Robinson, authors of "The 'Have-More' Plan." *Right.* A small silo made by the local blacksmith.

When the silo is full its contents should be leveled off and pressed down thoroughly and again in two days' time pressed down again and any spaces at the sides filled to exclude air. This pressing should be continued once a week until the material has settled evenly. The heaviest and greenest material, which dries more slowly, should be placed on top.

In removing for feeding, take pains to keep the material level and remove any that has spoiled, to prevent further rotting. Some will be messy on top. After opening for feeding it is well to continue to use the silage rapidly enough to prevent spoilage, as exposure to air each time will cause the material to deteriorate.

A small silo can be made from a molasses drum obtainable

from a bakery. A tight-fitting cover can be made from plywood—and adhesive tape may be used to fasten this to the drum and so seal silage from the air.

If your small silo is a success and the goats like the food—some will eat it, others perhaps refuse it—you may want to go into the making of it in quantities large enough to help out considerably with winter feeding and to provide yourself with more elaborate equipment. You can learn a lot about the making of silage from *Leaflet BDIM—Inf—38, USDA,* "Making Grass Silage by the Wilting Method," and *Farmers Bulletin No. 578 USDA,* "The Making and Feeding of Silage."

Another way of providing "silage" for your goats during the winter is simply to plant a small plot of sugar beets, mangels, or carrots. These may be stored in a root cellar. Goats will eat them with relish if they are washed and sliced.

Most small goatkeepers do not bother feeding silage. However, silage in the winter can mean more milk. If you get on the right side of your grocer he will save you lettuce leaves, cabbage leaves and carrot tops. Sometime in the near future it will be possible to buy canned silage from your feed man.

6

Grooming the Goat

PROBABLY every goat owner has met at one time or another the person who knows nothing about goats except that "they smell." My neighbor was most unhappy when he saw my goat barn going up. He believed that goats were noisy and smelly, but when the goats were installed he learned how mistaken he was, and has since brought many of his friends to see them. During the breeding season bucks do have an odor intended by nature to attract the does, which, while it isn't fragrant, need not be offensive if the bucks and their quarters are kept clean. Bucks form a very small percentage of the total number of goats, for most people with a few does do not keep a buck. To say that because the buck has an odor *goats* are smelly is just as unreasonable as to conclude that because a bull is dangerous cows are animals to be feared.

Female goats are most fastidious both regarding their food and themselves. They eat no animal food whatever and will roll their lips in disgust at the merest whiff of contaminated food. Although they might like the cookie or the apple that you offer, they won't take it if you have bitten into it. Nor will they eat food that another goat has mouthed. A goat can be housed in her stall for days, weeks, months and emerge with no unpleasant odor. Can this be said for a dog, a cat, horse, cow or any other domestic animal that you know?

The routine care of a goat is a simple matter. It means a good, brisk brushing of her coat each day, for which an ordinary coarse kitchen scrub brush is satisfactory. If this is done faithfully a goat will rarely develop lice or any unhealthy skin condition. Soiled spots, particularly if the goat is white, should be washed with warm, soapy water and the coat well dried. If the goat has long hair it is well to keep it trimmed around the flanks and the udder to make milking a clean process, and during warm weather the entire coat may be clipped with greater comfort to the animal.

From time to time, usually about once a month, it will be necessary to trim the goat's hoofs. If you are puzzled to know when hoofs are in need of trimming, look at the hoofs of a young kid, or when your goat first comes to you from the breeder look her hoofs over and see what well-cared-for hoofs look like. It is surprising how many people who otherwise take good care of their goats neglect this important detail. They seem to look upon it with a touch of dread—they might hurt her—but actually it is very easily done, and after one or two manicures the goat knows what to expect and rarely makes any protest. I have seen the hoofs of goats so overgrown that they looked like seashells. Ultimately, and quickly, this results in thickness and a malformation of the hoof that takes a long time to correct. Then, too, such neglect may result in hoof rot resulting from the packing of manure under the hoof. Particularly as a goat grows older her hoofs must be cared for, for, as with people, the feet of a goat sometimes get out of true and hoofs of this sort require more frequent trimming. I have a goat ten years old whose hoofs are as square and well formed as a kid's, but I also have a younger goat who tends to carry her weight on the side of her hoof, and who, as a consequence, needs more frequent treatment. You will find that the back hoofs, particularly, cannot stand neglect, and these by ill fortune are the more difficult to trim.

The supervision of the milkers' hoofs is easy, for the milking doe is on the bench each day and can be inspected often and quickly. The dry doe and the young stock, however, must not be overlooked.

Trimming the Goat's Hooves

Upper left. Use snap-type pruning shears. *Upper right.* Kid's hoof—the ideal to approach in trimming older goat's feet. *Lower.* The goat is easy to hold when fastened in milk stand.

The most comfortable place for such trimming is the milk bench. With the goat stanchioned, her movements are restricted and you can sit comfortably while doing the job. Start with the front hoof nearest you and with short pruning

59

shears or a short bladed knife trim off the excess rim, as you would a fingernail. If you use a knife, cut away from you and from the goat so that neither of you will be injured. Next, take the offside front hoof. You may draw this down under the goat's body at the side from which you milk her and where she is accustomed to find you, or if it is easier for you or for her, stand up with her body close against you and bend the leg at the knee, working from this angle.

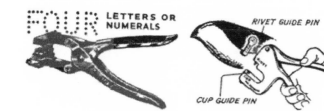

Three methods of identification

Tattoo marker. Ear tag. Notched ears.

In trimming the back hoofs stand with one foot on the bench and hold the back leg bent over your knee, grasping it at the ankle. If she attempts to kick allow her a little motion, but do not let her straighten her leg to its full length, and keep hold of the hoof. Talk to her quietly and in no time she will be quite under control. If the frog (the surface within the hoof rim) is thick and hard carefully trim that down, but be sure not to cut into the quick. The safe way is to cut a small sliver at a time and to stop before any pink shows. If the back part, the heel, seems thick and uneven that too should be trimmed, but sparingly.

That's all there is to it. It is just a matter of going slowly and carefully.

After a doe is bred it is well to cut her hoofs but as soon as she begins to grow heavy the manicures should be discontinued until after she has kidded, as too strenuous attempts to kick with those back legs might result in abortion.

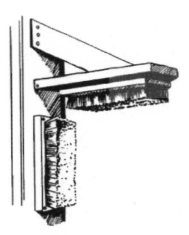

Nail two scrub brushes to a post in this fashion and goats will "curry" themselves.

7

Milking and Care of Milk and Equipment

MOST milking goats are milked twice a day, at intervals as nearly twelve hours apart as can be conveniently arranged. For such a task, repeated day after day, the right sort of equipment is essential. Otherwise it becomes irksome and what might be a pleasure becomes instead an irritating chore. With an expenditure of about ten dollars you can secure the equipment needed for milking and you would be wise to have it and to do the milking in a professional way. Your milk then will be as clean and wholesome as any dairy can produce, your disposition unruffled and time saved.

Instead of using that enamel kettle with only a small chip in it—which by the way can generate poisonous elements if used as a food container—get a seamless milking pail, preferably one with a hood to keep out particles of dirt and hairs; a milk strainer, and, for a larger dairy, a milk carrying pail (also seamless, which means no hiding place for bacteria). With the strainer you need a box of filter discs, made of sterilized cotton. One of these discs is clamped into the strainer for each milking—a fresh one each time.

It would be well also to have a strip cup. The first stream or two from the goat is milked into this cup which has at the top a very fine sieve. If the milk passing through the sieve leaves behind any lumps it usually means some unhealthy condition in the udder and such milk should not be used until the condition has been remedied.

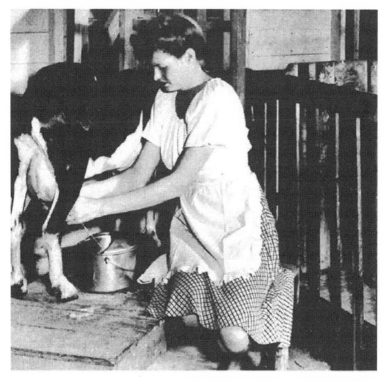

Milking a goat is not difficult. It is best done in a separate room. Note milk stand and covered pail.

As a check on yourself it is a good idea to have the milk

tested from time to time by your local board of health. Bring in a pint and they will send you a report of the bacteria count, the amount of butter fat, and the sediment, if any. The cost will probably be nothing, or too little to worry about. If the milk is below standard, the remedy is in your hands.

For the sake of cleanliness and comfort your goats should be milked on a bench, and does coming from a dairy herd have been trained to this routine. If your doe is a first milker or has not been accustomed to the bench you may need help to boost her onto the stand for the first milking or two, but she will learn readily. You may find it advisable to have a riser with a cleated surface so that the goat can walk up onto the stand, although most goats seem to like to jump up. It is all a matter of early training and the best plan is to continue in the way to which she has been accustomed.

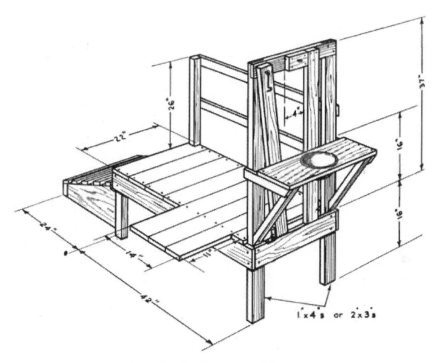

Details of milking stand for goat.

Have a shelf beside the bench and your equipment right at your elbow so that once you have started to milk you don't have to hop up for one thing or another. Brush the goat first, and don't neglect the under part of her body or the inner part of her hind legs. Wipe off her udder with a cloth wrung out of warm water to which you have added a few drops of chlorine solution, and dry her udder and your hands before proceeding to milk. A handy roll of paper towels is best for this—a clean, fresh towel for each goat. Be sure that your hands are clean,

65

and be careful not to touch the inside of the containers, otherwise your careful sterilizing will serve no purpose.

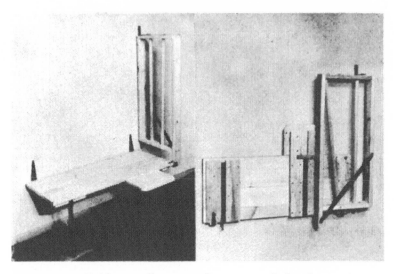

Folding milking stand—open and closed.

It is also well to keep in the barn a cotton frock with long sleeves such as grocers use which can be slipped on before the milking. Some health boards require that a band, or apron, be fixed about the goat's body to prevent hair from falling into the milk. You can make a simple apron from half a cotton grain bag without sewing a stitch. Just make a cut half way down each long side, about an inch or two in from the edge, tear a strip along the edge to about an inch from the end and tie a knot to prevent further tearing. This gives four tie strings. Pass two under the front legs and tie them across the goat's back; pass the other two under the hind legs and tie them across her back, over the hips.

If you can milk a cow, milking a goat will be easy for you, but if you have never milked before you will wonder how in the world with such a large container under the goat you can squirt the milk in so many different directions. The man from whom I purchased my goats supervised the making of the milking stand which had a rectangular platform on which the goat stood with head locked in place. I sat on the side and by the time I had finished milking there was milk up my sleeves, on my face and on the walls, and my legs ached from the strained position so that I could hardly keep from tears. The next time I tried sitting on a stool beside the bench. This was better, but too far away from the goat. Then came the happy thought of incorporating the seat with the platform. This was as it should have been from the start, but mine was the trial and error method. From then on the milking was no longer a torturing process and my aim was much surer. Once I had seen an Italian out in the pasture milk directly into a bottle, which seemed almost like magic, but soon I too could hit the bull's eye.

Here's how to milk: Sit on the milking stand facing the goat's udder, your shoulder close to her shoulder.

Encircle the teats, your thumbs outside your fingers. Close

your grasp, beginning at the top (thumb and index finger) and successively close the other fingers, thus forcing the milk down the teat and out in a steady stream. You will note that if you don't shut off the milk with your thumb and index finger, the milk will flow back into the udder when you squeeze with your second, third and little fingers. The motion of the fingers in milking is somewhat similar to playing the scale on the piano, except that the fingers are kept close together. That is the proper way to do it, but if you find it too difficult to operate each finger separately, pressing the teat with all the fingers at once will do.

The teats should be grasped and pressed alternately—not the udder—with as little motion as possible in the upper arm. The pressure should be firm but gentle. Pulling and stretching the udder may cause injury to delicate blood vessels. If the doe gets restless and moves her hind leg, protect the pail by pressure of your arm against her leg, and hold to the teat. If she moves her foreleg, pressure against it and against the under part of her body will control this. Sometimes a first freshener who has been nursing her kids will lie down on the bench to prevent being milked. A band passed under her forelegs and fastened over the front of the stanchion will keep her on her feet.

If your goat has been accustomed to being milked on the side opposite the side at which you milk, be patient with her until she becomes adjusted to the new position. At one time a doe was left with me for a week. Each time she was milked she tried to lie down. When her owner came I asked about this. He was puzzled. We put her on the bench to be milked and sure enough, down she went, even with her owner milking her. Then the light dawned and I asked, "On what side do you milk?" "The right," he said, and my bench was for left side milking.

Occasionally, particularly among Saanens, a young doe even before breeding, will develop milk in her udder—a virgin milker. If it seems necessary to relieve the pressure, she should be milked regularly.

When you think you have milked the goat out thoroughly, nudge her udder a few times and more milk will come, and lastly run your forefinger and thumb down the teat (this is called stripping) until you have gotten out the last drop. This isn't just Scotch thrift, but is necessary for thorough milking and keeps up the doe's production. Then, too, the milk that comes with stripping is the richest milk in her udder.

As soon as you have milked out the doe, pour the milk through the strainer, even before you return the milker to her stall, and when the milking is completed set the container in cold water—ice water if possible—as much water as you can use without tipping over the container. To ensure good flavor in milk and prevent the development of bacteria, rapid cooling is important, and cooling by immersion in cold water is a more rapid process than dry refrigeration. The milk should be brought down to a temperature of 50° F. within one hour after milking. Cubes from the refrigerator ice tray are fine to use, or if no ice is available change the water frequently as the warm milk will quickly raise its temperature.

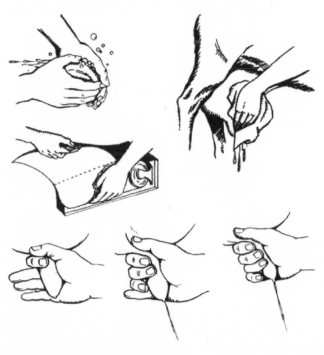

Upper left. In milking follow the same routine at each milking. Be gentle. Strangers—and the family dog tend to make a doe "hold up her milk." Keep them out of the barn or milk room. After milk pail and wash pail are ready, be sure your hands are clean. *Upper right.* Wash the goat's udder in chlorinated warm water—from 120°–130° F. The udder should be washed *just before milking*. Use a separate wash rag for each goat. *Center left.* Have a roll of paper towels handy to milking stand. Dry the goat's udder and your hands. Wet hands can cause a chapped udder—and worse. *Lower left.* Milk can run out of the teat into the pail or *back into the udder*. So first close your thumb and first finger so the milk can not run back into the udder. *Lower center.* Next close your second finger—and the milk should squirt out. Discard the first stream—it will be high in bacteria. *Lower right.* Close the third finger. Use a steady pressure. Don't jerk down.

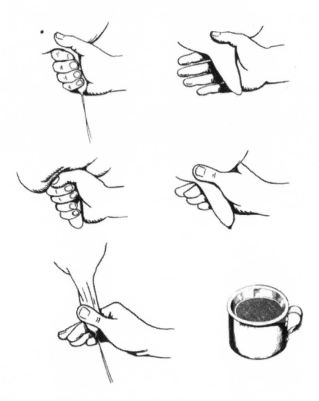

Upper left. Next close your little finger . . . squeeze with whole hand. *Upper right.* Now release the teat and let it fill up with milk. Repeat the process with the other hand . . . *Center left.* When the milk flow is near to stopping, nudge the bag to see if the doe has let down all her milk. *Center right.* The final bit of milk may be stripped out. Take teat between thumb and first finger. *Lower left.* Now run down length of teat. Milk high in butter fat usually comes at end of milking. But prolonged stripping is bad for the teats and udder. *Lower right.* Strip cup: the first milk is milked into the strip cup. If the milk is "lumpy" it will not pass through the strainer.

When the milk is cooled it may be transferred to bottles, capped and placed in the refrigerator. Gallon glass jars (such as are used for mayonnaise), or quart canning jars make excellent milk containers and are much easier to clean than the customary milk bottle. As the milk is used the metal cap which screws on the outside of the jar can be removed and replaced with less danger of contaminating the milk than with the reused bottle cap made of cardboard. The lining, of course, should be removed from the cap, and a piece of waxed paper may be used in its place to protect the milk from splashing against the metal cover.

All milking equipment should be rinsed in cold water immediately after use then washed in warm, soapy water to which chlorine solution is added. This solution is available at your grain dealer's, or you can make it yourself by dissolving one 12-ounce can of chloride of lime in a gallon of cold water. After the lime has settled pour the water into bottles. Add this solution to your wash water in the proportion of 4 tablespoons of the chlorine to 3 gallons of water. Finally the utensils should be rinsed in boiling water and set in a dust free place to dry by evaporation. As a further precaution this last step may be repeated just prior to milking for the extremely hot water will dry the utensils very quickly.

Don't leave milk to sun itself on the kitchen table, but be sure that it is kept always in the refrigerator, properly capped. Don't set a pitcher of milk on the shelf uncovered and then blame your goat for off-flavored milk if it doesn't taste good to you. Raw milk absorbs flavors very quickly, and must at all times be kept covered.

8

Breeding—Good and Bad

THE lactation period of most does lasts from eight to ten months after freshening, although it is not unusual for a doe to continue milking for a year or more. The breeding season, however, is limited to the fall and winter months. Does come in heat from September through March, with occasionally a doe ready for breeding in August, and on rare occasions even in July with Nubians. For this reason most goat owners breed yearly to be sure that a doe does not go dry during the months when normally they do not come in heat. If you have two does, their breeding can be so spaced as to keep you supplied with a continuous flow of milk over the year. The first breeding may be in August or September so that the doe will freshen five months later, in January or February; the second doe bred in November or December, to freshen in May or June. This will give you the heaviest supply of milk during the summer months when more milk is consumed, but will keep some milk available even during the cold months, which is an important matter if the milk is used for infant feeding.

The indications of a doe in heat are several, although all may not be evident in a particular doe and it is sometimes difficult for the novice to recognize them. Perhaps the most noticeable is a continuous twitching of the tail which becomes more pronounced if the hand is passed along the doe's back. With this may go a loss of appetite, bleating, redness and swelling around the vulva and sometimes a mucous discharge. A doe in heat is apt to annoy her companion goats by rubbing against them. Watch for these indications with the coming of fall and if you desire to breed the doe hustle her off to a buck, which you have previously located, without delay. Although the heat period may last two or three days, it may also last but a few hours. If you are not prepared to breed her, she will again come in heat in twenty-one days (sometimes sooner) until bred. When you take her to the buck don't just leave her and go off on other business. Actual mating takes less than a minute, and it is better to wait and be sure that she is served and then take her away. Repeated service is of no benefit to the doe and a distinct disadvantage to the buck—a waste of energy.

This common goat, of little value as a milker, was bred to a purebred Saanen Buck. Her daughter (lower opposite page), is a half blood. Again a pure-bred sire was used. Here you see the result—a 3/4 blood. Notice the improvement in type.

When the doe has been served, she will indicate it by arching her body and perhaps giving off a mucouslike discharge. Make a record of the date and watch for a return of the heat symptoms in twenty-one days, or even sooner. Recurrence of these would indicate that the doe is *not* pregnant and service should be repeated. If in twenty-one days she does not come in heat, it is safe to assume that she is bred. Within a month or two she will show definite signs of being with kid. Count off five months (146–153 days) from the date of service and make a record of this, too, as the date on which the kids should be born.

Sometimes, for some inexplicable reason, a doe does not seem to come in heat. This occurred with a doe brought to me for service in February. All season she had apparently not come in heat and her owner was concerned that breeding might be missed. The doe was taken to the buck each day for several weeks, but showed no interest in him. At the end of March the veterinarian inoculated her with stilbesterol. The following day she was very obviously in heat and was served by the buck. On the other hand, late in April a man hurried over with a doe to be bred. He was sure that she was in heat—her tail twitched constantly. Although doubtful, since the season was so late, I took her to the buck without result. Probably the tail twitching was due to the irritation of tiny gnats that come so often with the early spring days. However, we did discover that she had a plentiful supply of lice and suggested treatment so that the trip wasn't wholly a futile one.

Opinions differ as to the best age for breeding young stock, some breeders advocating early breeding if the doe is well developed and vigorous. Others prefer to wait until she is in her second year—about eighteen months old, so that she will be two years old at the time of first freshening.

Inbreeding—the mating of does and bucks of the same blood, such as father and daughter, mother and son, brother and sister—and linebreeding (the mating of closely related animals, but showing unrelated blood in either parent, such as grandfather and granddaughter sired by an unrelated buck, or grandmother and grandson whose dam is of another strain) are branches of breeding that the amateur would best leave to the experienced breeder. It requires scientific knowledge of the laws of breeding and heredity, keen observation and understanding of the good and bad points of the animals involved, time and money to pursue them. Such breeding naturally results in concentration of certain characteristics possessed by the strain, but one may only succeed in emphasizing unsuspected weaknesses that would have been offset with outbreeding.

It is desirable, however, that your doe be mated to a buck of her same breed, and you should select the buck with the same care as you would use in purchasing an animal. See what his background is, what kind of daughters he has produced, and if he is healthy and vigorous himself. Too many people undo the work of years of conscientious effort on the part of good breeders by taking their does to the nearest buck with the explanation that they just want to freshen them. Later, the appeal of the doe kids is so strong that they either retain them or give them to some friend who might better have had a kid with the true characteristics of the mother's breed, not just a little mongrel, however lovable. With a registered buck of the mother's breed as her sire, the little doe should be a step ahead of her mother in appearance and production.

After breeding, the milking doe will gradually give less and less milk until after three months you will probably find it unnecessary to milk her. If, however, she continues to produce milk she should be dried off. This may be done gradually by omitting the evening milking, then milking every other day, then increasing the intervals between milking until the flow of milk has ceased. Or it may be done abruptly by just not milking the doe. In following the latter method it is necessary to give careful attention to her udder and to milk it out if necessary to give her relief in case it becomes crowded with milk. Occasionally, a doe who is a very heavy milker is difficult to dry off, but it must be done, for a twenty-four hour shift producing milk and nourishing her unborn kids is too severe a strain on the prospective mother and likely to end unhappily.

When the doe has been dried off, a fitting ration (obtainable from most grain companies) should be fed, or the usual grain ration should be lessened gradually and augmented with bran to supply bulk, so that by the time of kidding the doe is getting about half bran in her grain allowance. The hay feeding should be generous, but a leaner hay than alfalfa or clover used. She should have warm water two or three times daily. Her daily exercise should be continued, but care must be taken to protect her from incidents that might frighten her and cause running or bumping. A gentle word and her name spoken is often all that is required to calm a nervous doe.

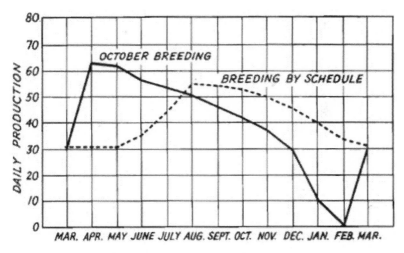

Breed for Continuous Production

The goat industry's greatest practical difficulty is probably the seasonal breeding period. The normal breeding season is from Aug.–Jan. About 3/4 of the goats in the U.S. are bred in the months of Sept., Oct., and Nov. and freshen in Feb., Mar., and April. Thus, production during late fall and early winter in most herds is very low. This is a serious handicap for any dairy in building a group of permanent customers.

Although the Dept. of Agr. at Beltsville, Md., has had some success in overcoming this problem by the use of hormones, no complete solution has been found. There does appear to be a greater than average range in the breeding season for Nubians.

In spite of this handicap much can be done through careful planning to smooth out the seasonal production curve of a herd. The graph illustrates these possibilities. The solid line represents production for a herd in which all goats are bred around Oct. 1, making them freshen in early Mar.

The following plan could be followed:

1. Breed 1/4 of the herd as soon as possible—by Sept. 1 to freshen before Feb. 1.

2. Breed 1/4 (the least persistent producers of those left) in Oct. to freshen in Mar.

3. Breed 1/4 (persistent producers) in Nov. to freshen in

April.

4. Breed 1/4 (persistent producers) after Dec. 15 to freshen in late May or early June.

Groups 3 and 4 would give considerable milk during the usual months of shortage and would not dry off until after Group 1 had freshened. Such a breeding schedule would give a herd production curve similar to the broken line in the graph. A sizeable production would be secured even in the months of Dec., Jan., and Feb. This would be of great help in building a permanent trade.

9

The Buck

WILL you need a buck?

If the herd is small, say less than ten or a dozen does, it is hardly advisable to have a buck, unless you live in an isolated section and can find no good buck of the same breed as your does available. With the exception that he doesn't need to be milked, the buck must receive the same care as the does. He must have his own quarters, weatherproof, well-lighted and comfortable, and far enough removed from the does so that he is not disturbed during the breeding season by their nearness. He should have his own exercise yard.

The buck needs brushing, hoof trimming, an occasional washing, regular feeding and watering just as the does do, and his pen must be cleaned regularly. People are oftentimes inclined to neglect the buck, giving him scant attention aside from his feeding, which has much to do with the reputation he gets of being an evil-smelling creature. There is no denying that even the best kept bucks have an odor, especially insistent during the mating season, but with reasonable care this may be kept to an inoffensive minimum—certainly much below the mark which announces his presence 100 yards away.

If you intend to go in for goat breeding you will, of course, need your own buck. Whether your does are grades or purebreds, the buck should be a registered animal. Only with such a sire can you hope to retain the breed characteristics of your stock and improve it with each generation. You may prefer to purchase a mature buck who has given proof of his ability to produce daughters that are good milkers, or you may secure a buck kid and raise him yourself. For women goatkeepers the latter is the better plan for the young buck can be brought up in kindly fashion so that he will be easy to manage at all times.

In selecting a buck kid use the same precautions as in the selection of your does. Scrutinize his blood lines carefully and his immediate family—dam, sire and sisters if possible. Select a kid with good bone structure and a good, broad chest. Even a young buck will show quality if he has it. The price of a buck kid is, naturally, much less than that of a mature, proven buck. You do take some chance as to his potency, but a buck kid matures rapidly, and at six months is old enough for limited service. The chance is worth taking, for the molding of the buck's disposition is entirely in your hands. To my mind a buck who must be approached with pitchfork in hand or who wears a ring in his nose is proof of improper early handling, for goats are almost without exception fond of people and very responsive to kind treatment.

When the first milker I had, a Toggenburg doe, was ready for breeding I located a topnotch Toggenburg buck for service. A transcript of his pedigree was sent and I went to see him. I was taken into the barn and in the far end, amid a great rattling of chains, a very impressive looking animal was lowered on a platform. I stood back in fear—it was like a visit to the Spanish Inquisition. The buck was a fine animal and my doe was bred, but I stayed securely in the car until she was brought out to me.

When my herd was large enough to need a buck I secured a three-year-old. Later I learned that his owner had been afraid of him and he too had kept the buck chained at all times. As a result he didn't trust people and could never be fully trusted himself nor allowed complete freedom. He had a good-sized corral, but when he grazed in the open he had to be tied. Before venturing into his pen I always tied him at the far end of the corral. While he never injured anyone, he frightened a good many and he always required a watchful eye. Many times when I brushed him, although he liked to be brushed, he would send the brush hurtling through the air.

Toggenburg buck

Since then I have raised several buck kids and not one has shown a disposition to be anything but gentle and friendly. Perhaps I have just been lucky, but I have known several women who have handled their own bucks and all have had the same good fortune. My present buck, now in his fourth year, is given complete freedom whenever possible. In good weather the door of his house is open and he can come and go in the field at any time when the does are not there. When they are in the field he is closed in his own yard. As soon as he hears me moving about in the morning, he comes down along the fence and calls. Whenever I want him I call his name and he answers or comes to see what is wanted. He receives the same care as the does—is fed and watered regularly, brushed, washed on occasion, his hoofs trimmed and his head scratched when he invites it. After a doe is served she is taken away immediately—a severe test of a buck's amiability—and he makes no protest. He does not live in lonely solitude, but has a wether (a castrated buck) of his own age for companion, brought up with him from baby days. Because he is not obliged to live in loneliness, he is quite devoid of the objectionable habits so often found in bucks. At times he and the wether have their differences, usually during the breeding season, but their house has two pens separated by a solid partition with a drop gate and, when it seems advisable, the gate is put in place and they are separated, yet side by side for companionship. When morning comes, they are once more good friends and glad to be together in the field.

Nubian buck

If you decide on a buck kid be careful that he does not remain too long with the does or doe kids. As soon as he begins to get "bucky" give him his own quarters, for at three months of age a young buck is a potential father. But give him a playmate, or let him spend as much time as possible in your company. Do not, however, play with him or allow the children or the dog to push him about. It is amusing to see these kids rear up and butt in play, but it ruins them for later handling. You may train the buck to harness and use him for hauling manure, grass cutting and other work. It's good exercise for him—but he must respect you—and he won't if you become his playmate. Work quietly about him and don't startle him— always speak to him when you come into his house, and never beat him. A goat cannot be trained with the lash as can a dog into a cowering creature. He can just be made treacherous by such handling.

Saanen buck

During the first season the young buck should be used only infrequently for service with long rest periods between matings. An older buck can serve thirty or more does during a season and still keep in excellent condition if the breedings are distributed fairly evenly through the breeding months and limited to two a day. He should be well fed with plenty of good hay and a daily ration of grain, a pound or more, depending on your own observation of his body needs—enough to keep him in good flesh but not fat.

90

A young buck or wether may be trained to harness.

10

Kidding

THE normal gestation period of a goat—i.e. the period during which she carries her young—is 150 days. Sometimes the kids are dropped a few days early, sometimes a few days late.

Some weeks before the kids are due, if the doe has been kept in a tie stall, it is well to remove her to her kidding pen so that she may move about freely. Have the pen clean and well bedded. Several weeks before the kids are born she will show a noticeable depression at either side of her tail and a hollowness at the hip bones. Her udder will fill, gradually at first, then toward the end rather rapidly. Feel the udder from time to time and should it become hard and shiny it may be necessary to milk out a small quantity of milk. So long as the udder is flexible, no milk need be removed.

A day or two before kidding the doe will become restless, lying down and getting up frequently, arranging her bedding and talking to you. There may be a mucous discharge for a day or two which just before kidding will become heavy and gelatinous. Have your equipment ready and convenient—newspaper and towels for drying off the kids, boric acid powder, sterilized scissors and a deep box or carton well bedded with hay or straw or even strips of newspaper in which to place the kids; a basin, bar of soap, a soft wash cloth and soft towel for the mother. Daytime kidding is a great relief, but even if it means sacrificing your sleep, plan to be on hand at the time of birth. It will give the doe confidence if she is nervous, and you will be ready to give assistance if necessary. Nine times out of ten no help will be needed.

*"Capricious" comes from capra originally a fantastic goat leap—
but only those who have watched kids at play grasp the full
meaning of this word.*

93

Saanen Kid just born.

Saanen Kid just 10 minutes old!

In a normal birth the front hoofs of the kid will show first with the head between. When the kid's head emerges fully break the sac in which it is enclosed so that it can breathe and wipe the mucous from its nose and mouth. You may help the mother, if she needs help, by pressing on her sides as her body contracts, and you may grasp the head of the kid and help to ease it out with the mother's efforts, but do not pull the kid from her. Such haste may result in hemmorhage.

95

Usually the cord attaching the kid to the mother breaks of itself, but it may be necessary to use your small scissors. Snip it several inches from the kid's stomach and tie with a soft cord two or three inches from the navel. Be careful not to tie the cord so tightly that the tissue is cut. Sometimes it is advisable to place a tight sterile binder around the kid's body.

The second kid usually follows in a few minutes, although I have had a doe whose second kid was born eight hours after the first. Sometimes there are three kids, or even four.

After a half hour, if the mother seems comfortable and free from pain it is fairly safe to assume that there will be no more kids. She may then be given a dish of bran mixed with quite warm water, moist but not wet, a drink of warm water and a supply of fresh hay. Then the kid can be attended to—dried off so that her hair is soft and fluffy, the navel dusted with boric acid powder and the kid placed back in her box. If the barn is cold pin old blankets around the stall to protect the mother and kid.

Sometimes the kid will come hind legs first—a little more difficult birth for the mother, but not alarming. And again a kid may be crosswise in the uterus and need to be turned before it can be born. If you do this turning yourself, be sure that your nails are clean and your hands sterilized or that you use a rubber glove, and be very gentle. Also it may be, more rarely, that there is a dead kid which the mother cannot expel. In this event it is wise to have the services of a veterinarian unless you are confident of your own ability to cope with the matter.

Quadruplets!

After the kids are born make the mother comfortable by removing the soiled bedding and putting down a clean layer. But do not disturb her to the point of a complete cleaning of her pen at this time. Wash her udder with warm, soapy water and dry it with the soft towel. She is then ready to be milked or to feed her kids.

The waste matter, or afterbirth, may come from the mother a half hour or so after kidding. If it does, thank Lady Luck and go about other duties with a feeling of relief, for the kids can wait some hours if necessary for their first feeding. It more often happens, however, that it is several hours before the afterbirth is expelled, and as some does are inclined to eat the afterbirth it is well to check on the mother from time to time so that you may dispose of it when it is free. But here again, do not pull it from the mother. Give nature a chance to do the job unassisted. If the mother eats the afterbirth the most serious effect seems to be a lack of interest in her food for a day or two which can often be corrected with a warm drink to which bicarbonate of soda is added.

One of the astonishing things about new born kids is the fact that often as soon as they are dried off, about a minute after birth, they stand up and walk. Unlike a number of other animals—puppies and rabbits, for instance, kids come into the world fully equipped—eyes wide open, tiny teeth, and muscles well coordinated. And there isn't any animal more appealing than a frisky, two-days-old kid.

11

Feeding the Kids

NEWBORN KIDS may be left with the mother to get their milk directly from her udder, or they may be hand fed by bottle or pan. Most people prefer pan feeding. It takes less time, there is no breakage or tearing of rubber nipples, and the pans are more easily cleaned than the bottles.

Make your decision about the method you will use before the kids are born. It is extremely difficult to change a kid's feeding habit after she has had her first milk from the original source. Some people leave the kids with the mother for the first few feedings, to be sure that they get the colostrum, the first milk, and then shift to pan or bottle feeding, but my experience with this method has brought plenty of headaches.

I purchased a week-old buck, nursed by his mother, and spent hours trying to feed him from a pan with dismal, heartbreaking failure. Then I tried a baby's nursing bottle, holding it in his mouth and tilting his head so that gravity forced him to swallow. He was a beautiful, large kid, but grew thin and developed diarrhea, and was most forlorn. Finally I put a fresh doe on the bench and held her teat in his mouth, gently squeezing the milk into his mouth. He took it eagerly.

By holding my hand on the doe's udder she thought that I was milking her and we all got on nicely, but I never could get that kid to feed from a pan or bottle.

If the kids are does and the goat milk is needed for human food it is best to hand feed them. Thus the supply of milk can be controlled and after three or four weeks on mother's milk they may be fed a substitute. Hand feeding has the added advantage that the kids are ready for sale and their feeding no problem to their new owner.

Where the milk supply is not needed, it's easiest to let the kids nurse. Breeders who don't sell milk usually follow this method.

As soon as the newborn kid begins to nudge around its mother and would seem to be ready for food place your milk container in a pan of quite warm water and milk about a half-pint into it. Transfer this to a measuring cup, also warm, or if the doe is accustomed to being milked and will stand quiet, and your aim is good, set the measuring cup in the warm water and milk directly into it. Feed this to the kid at once, while quite warm. It should be 100° F. and you should use a thermometer for accuracy. You will find that the small circumference of the cup helps to keep the kid's head over the milk and she will drink it down to the last drop. With a larger container she is apt to lose her place and grope about desperately, splashing and spilling the milk. In a week's time you may use a pan with better success.

If goat milk is being used by the family—or sold—it's best to teach kids to drink from a pan. Skim milk or "calf" starter may be substituted for whole milk.

A little kid is sometimes slow in taking her first feeding. If she isn't disposed to take the milk, cool it and place it in the refrigerator. In an hour or two reheat the milk to 100° F. and try again. Don't throw this first milk away for it contains properties very essential for cleansing the intestinal tract of the kid and antibodies to protect it from disease. It is a yellow milk sometimes quite thick and you may find when you are ready to use it again that you will need to thin it with boiled (not boiling) water. Be very careful in heating this colostrum milk and don't place it over direct heat. It is best to set your container in hot water and watch it closely. Too much heat will cause the milk to set like custard so that it cannot be used.

Unfortunately, little buck kids, unless they are of excellent breeding and are to be used for herd sires, seem to have no place in the world. They may be raised for driving goats or for pets, but oftentimes as they grow older their lot in life isn't a happy one. They are given to this one or that one, neglected and at times even abused. They are so intelligent and sweet that it is hard to think of butchering them, but it would seem that they are destined for food. The simplest and least troublesome way of feeding these kids is to leave them with the mother to help themselves. It is not safe, however, to assume that they are taking all the milk the mother is producing, especially during the first few days, and each day any excess should be milked out to avoid udder trouble and to keep up the doe's production. Also to prevent a lop-sided development of the udder, see that the kids take the milk from both sides.

By the time the buck kids are four to eight weeks old they are ready for butchering, and particularly if available at Easter-time there is a market waiting for them at a price ranging from $5 up, depending on their age and the demand. People who buy these buck kids for food prefer that they be milk fed exclusively—no hay or grain permitted—although there is no insistence that they be castrated. However, if after eight weeks they have not been sold it is wise to have them castrated, particularly if they are kept with the does or young doe kids, for they show an early interest in the does and even at three months are *capable of service*.

The most commonly used substitute for natural goat milk in kid feeding is powdered skim milk. The powder is added to cold water—3/4 cup to a quart—and mixed with a rotary egg beater. This remade milk should be added to goat milk and introduced to the kid gradually, the amount of goat milk reduced and the skim milk increased each day until the goat milk has been wholly eliminated, if none can be spared for the kid's feeding.

Kids may also be fed by bottle. The milk should be warmed to prevent scours.

For the first few weeks the kid should be fed frequently, at least four times daily, a half-pint at a feeding. Remember, the milk should be warm. When the kid takes her feedings eagerly they may be reduced to three daily and the amount increased. At about a week old the kid will begin to nibble at hay and it should be kept constantly before her, preferably at a little height above her head so that she must reach for it.

104

Also at about this time try her with a fine grain mixture such as calf starter. As her appetite for hay and grain increases her milk feedings may be reduced to two a day and at three or four months may be discontinued entirely. A salt brick should be handy for her to lick. She should be given warm water, but not left to take her fill of it. Kids are greedy little creatures and will drink to the bursting point unless supervised.

Always have the utensils for the kid feeding clean, the milk warm and the bedding dry—which means frequent changing for kids do a great deal of wetting. Give them opportunity for exercise—a box or platform to jump on—fresh air and sunshine, and keep them warm, and they will be strong and healthy.

12

Removing Horns

ALTHOUGH a goat with horns is oftentimes a very beautiful animal, there is always the possibility of injury to her handler or to other goats from her horns, even though her disposition is of the sweetest. There was a time when goat breeders were disposed to destroy kids born with horns and many good milkers were probably thus lost. Now the theory is that horns are evidence of virility and their removal is so simple and safe a procedure that there is no thought of destroying the kids.

Statistics on hermaphrodites—animals with the sex organs of both female and male—in the government experimental herd at Beltsville, Md. show that such animals were invariably the result of mating polled (naturally hornless) bucks and does, and were not found among the offspring of horned parents. It is suggested that in their efforts to breed naturally hornless animals, goat breeders may be building for themselves a more serious problem—the production of hermaphrodites of no productive value.

As you dry off the kid you may notice two little swirls of hair over the eyes, where horns appear on older goats. These usually mean a horned kid, but don't jump to a hasty conclusion. When the kid is three or four days old you can make sure by cutting with small curved scissors the hair close to the skin. Then try to move the skin back and forth over the little nubble. If it moves freely the kid will be hornless. If the skin is tight at this spot she will have horns—that is she will unless you take steps to check their growth. This should be done while the kid is still very young, before the horns break through, before the kid is a week old.

Natural growth of horns.

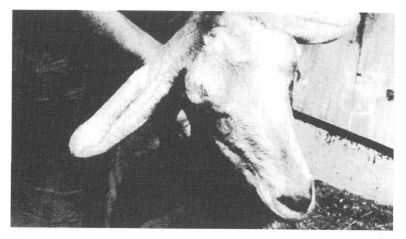

This goat's horns were removed by caustic potash when she was a three-day-old kid.

There are several methods for stopping the development of horns. An electric dehorning iron may be used—placed over the horn button after the hair has been closely clipped, and the horn bud burned by the electric current, or an iron, similar in appearance but heated to white heat may be used.

There are pastes, applied according to directions given by the manufacturer, and there is the inexpensive and effective method—the use of caustic potash. In using the potash the procedure is as follows:

Clip the hair closely over and around the horn button over a surface about the size of a quarter, large enough so that you can see easily what you are doing. Cover the bared surface temporarily with a disc of adhesive tape and smear around the edges with vaseline so that the caustic will burn only the spot where you want it to burn. Hobble the hind legs of the kid, allowing enough freedom so that she can walk about, but cannot bring her hind leg forward to scratch the spot where the potash is applied, which she will immediately try to do when she feels the sting. Use a stick of potash about the thickness of a crayon, wetting the end on blotting paper. Have it just moist, not running wet. Remove the piece of tape and apply the potash back and forth on the horn button until little blisters appear, but not enough to cause bleeding. Be sure to wrap the end of the stick held in your hand with a non-absorbent material such as tinfoil for it will burn your fingers as well as the kid's skin. After the job is completed, hold the kid quiet for a few moments so that she won't rub the wet spot. She may then be allowed to run about and seems to notice the pain less if she is active, but she must be watched as she may attempt to rub her head against another kid or wherever she can to allay the burning sensation. Within a half hour or so she will cease to feel the pain.

Disbudding horns by use of caustic potash

Upper left. Clip hair around horn button. Upper right. Cut two pieces of adhesive tape large enough to cover horn button. Lower left. Apply vaseline around adhesive. Lower right. Remove adhesive; apply caustic.

Of course it takes two people to do this—one to hold the kid firmly keeping her head steady so that neither the scissors nor the potash comes near her eyes. Be very careful in using the potash as a trickle running down into the hair may result in blindness or disfigurement.

111

For removing horns after they have developed there are several methods. The horns may be sawed off about two inches from their base very evenly with no ugly appearance resulting. And there is the complete dehorning of the mature animal. This is really a major operation and should be done only by a veterinarian, if at all. It is very bloody and very painful, a severe shock to the animal.

Many people report good results through the use of rubber bands. The hair is clipped close to the head, two little notches filed in the horn, and a rubber band wound around the horn as near as possible to the base, held secure with adhesive tape. It may be necessary to replace the band from time to time as the rubber loses its elasticity or breaks. This band stops the circulation of blood at the root of the horn and in about six weeks the horn drops off. Various results have been reported from this method, some people finding that the goat appeared to suffer no discomfort, but occasionally someone finding that the horn became infected or the goat suffered such pain that the band had to be removed.

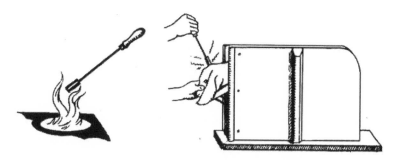

Left. Disbudding iron. Right. Kid-holding stall.

With Nubians, whose horns are flat and rather short, I have found it quite sufficient to wrap adhesive tape around the tip of the horn, forming a cushion so that the pointed end is rounded and in the event that the horned goat does butt another there is no danger of the horn tip puncturing or seriously harming the other animal. The tape will stay on for months and can easily be replaced when it becomes soiled, and this gives the goat no discomfort whatever.

13

Chevon

IF YOU intend to keep buck kids for food they should be castrated at an early age. After eight weeks they mature rapidly and unless castrated will be an annoyance to the young does and a source of worry to you, with the growing possibility of the premature breeding of a very young doe kid. After they have been castrated they may mingle freely with the rest of the herd for an indefinite time—until such time as it is desired to slaughter them. Although the meat of the young kids is considered a delicacy comparable to baby lamb, the castrated male, or wether, makes excellent food at any age. If you have facilities for freezing, the kids may be prepared while young and kept in the freezer until needed.

There are three generally used methods of castrating. A device may be obtained from veterinary supply houses for the purpose, with instructions for its use, which requires no cutting. There is the surgical method in which the scrotum or sac which encloses the testicles, is cut at the base, about an inch removed, and the testicles pressed through and withdrawn until the cord breaks. The wound is then dusted with an antiseptic powder such as boric acid and the kid kept quiet in clean quarters, warm and dry for a few days. When properly done this is not a bloody operation and the kid recovers from it fairly quickly, some kids not even missing a single meal. More recently many people have found the use of a rubber band simple, apparently quite painless and generally successful. With this method the band is wound around the scrotum, close to the body as soon after birth as the testicles have come into place. The band cuts off the circulation of blood into the organs and prevents their development.

Upper. In castrating a buck, swab the side of scrotum where incisions are to be made with a germicide. Lower. the operation may be done on a milking stand or the buck held in this position. Note how first incision is made.

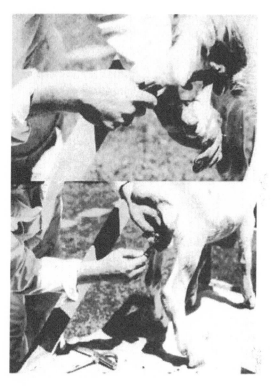

Upper. Two incisions are made. One testicle at a time is squeezed outside sack and the cord cut. Lower. A germicide is applied after both testicles are removed.

When performed with skill, the pain is so slight that, as in this case, the buck continues to eat grain throughout the operation without bleating.

The first kids I had castrated were done by an Italian who had had goats in the old country. He used a method similar to the rubber band method, except that he used a willow twig and a soft twine, and he waited for a new moon before he would do the work. The moon was auspicious and the results successful, although the method is primitive and not to be

118

recommended.

In performing any of these operations it is, of course, necessary that some person hold the kid firmly to prevent struggling and that the hands of the worker and the implements used be sterilized to prevent infection. Although the bucks may be castrated at any age it is advisable that it be done while they are young. With older bucks the risk is greater and the results less satisfactory.

The meat of the goat, called chevon, especially that of the young kids, is much desired at the Easter season by people of foreign birth, and in fact the kids are readily saleable to them at any season. In flavor it is similar to lamb and may be cooked in any way in which lamb is used.

If you have raised the kid yourself, without being sentimental about it, you may find it difficult to do the butchering, as the little buck kids are as appealing as the does and although you may fully intend to be indifferent to them they will not be ignored. One tries to think of them as of baby pigs, or lambs, or chickens, but can't, for they have an innate trust in human beings and an intelligence not equalled by any other young domestic animal, not even puppies. If you can harden yourself to doing the butchering there is an excellent, clear, simple, well illustrated booklet issued by the *Dairy Goat Journal*, Columbia, Missouri, called "Butchering, Chevon, and Goat Hides," which tells in detail how to go about it. People accustomed to farm life are more practical about these matters, and if you shrink from doing the butchering it is not difficult to find a farmer experienced in slaughtering lambs or other livestock who will do the butchering and dressing for you.

For years I found it impossible to reconcile myself to the butchering of kids and tried instead to raise them for pets. Two little bucks, Pete and Bunty, beautifully matched, went off to delighted children, but one day I met the village hermit dragging them along through the rain. The children had taken them out and neglected to return them to their pen and they had eaten the prize roses. The old hermit smelled strongly of whiskey and I had doubts about the skill with which he would do his killing so I paid for the kids and brought them back. Then they were given to a little boy who loved them through the summer months, but when fall came he had to return to the city and the kids were brought back again. Finally they went into other hands for driving goats, but with the meat shortage they too very likely found their way to the table.

Another little buck was ordered for a pet, together with his sister. On returning one day to the barn I found them both back in the pasture and a note which read "We find they require too much care and are returning them. Will charge it up to experience."

Marcy Boy, a little wether, was purchased for a pet. Driving through the back roads one day I noticed a forlorn little scrawny kid beside a tumble-down house. Marcy Boy had been given away, and when I asked the children what they fed him they answered, "He's so fussy. He won't eat things." There were chickens running about and I suggested that he be given some of the chicken feed in a clean pan and I thought he'd eat it.

These and other unhappy experiences convinced me finally that early butchering is after all the most humane disposition of these little bucks not needed for service.

14

Keeping Goats Healthy

IF YOU have read much about goats you have probably met time and time again the statement that goats are the healthiest of domestic animals. This does not, however, justify their neglect nor the thought that they can be left entirely on their own and come out on top. Goats are healthy, but only if they are cared for and given good food. In damp and drafty quarters, or left out in storms or cold winds with no shelter they have every chance to develop pneumonia, and it is pretty hard to save the life of a goat with this disease. If by some unfortunate chance a goat gets chilled, a good brisk rubbing is in order, a woolen sweater or blanket, and a warm drink. If she won't take the water, add molasses or something sweet to make it inviting, or try warm goat milk or even black coffee, and give her a warm bran mash. If she doesn't improve promptly have the veterinarian without delay.

Another unwholesome condition to which goats are prone is worms, and these, too, may prove fatal. There is a large variety of worms to which both sheep and goats are susceptible and their cause is chiefly too concentrated pasturing. Consequently, when goats are wormed they should be given a fresh pasture or the pasture treated so that the larvae are destroyed. Your State Department of Agriculture will advise you as to the most up-to-date chemical to use as well as how long it will be before goats can be returned to a pasture so treated.

Noticeable indications of worms in a goat are loss of appetite, thinness, pale eye and mouth membranes, rough coat, and soft droppings. A specimen of the droppings may be sent to your own state experiment station or college of agriculture for analysis to confirm any suspicion you may have that your goats are wormy.

For some years the most effective treatment employed for worms in sheep and goats was a drench of copper sulphate solution, but more recently the approved treatment is the use of phenothiazine. The copper sulphate required the fasting of the animal and was dangerous to administer because it had to be given as a drench. The phenothiazine may be given as a powder in the food, requires no preliminary fasting; some goats will eat it with their grain unsuspectingly, but some will not touch the feed. If liquid phenothiazine or phenite is used it may be administered with a bulb syringe or the pellet form can be placed down the throat. If you can get your hands on what is known as a small "balling gun" the pellet will go down more easily.

The United States Department of Agriculture in an

article "Phenothiazine for the Control of Parasites of Farm Animals" states that this drug is effective against such worms as common stomach worms, lesser stomach worms, bankrupt worms, hookworms, large-mouthed bowel worms, and also nodular worms for which previously no effective treatment had been found. The dosage for a mature goat is 20 grams (4/5 of an ounce). For animals weighing 60 pounds 12 grams is sufficient. As a preventive two treatments a year are considered adequate—in the fall and in the spring before the animals go out to pasture. The advisability of administering drugs to pregnant animals is always questionable, and recent experiments have shown that dosing does pregnant more than two months may cause them to abort. Dosing during the first two months of pregnancy is less risky. The one disadvantage in the use of phenothiazine is that it turns the milk pink for three or four days and unusable as human food. However, the treatment of the animals may be so arranged that but one milker at a time need be treated. If the dry goats and the milkers are pastured in separate enclosures, a trough may be placed for the dry stock in which a mixture of phenothiazine and granular, loose salt is available at all times—nine parts salt to one part powdered phenothiazine, by weight. Then the semi-yearly treatment may be omitted for the dry stock.

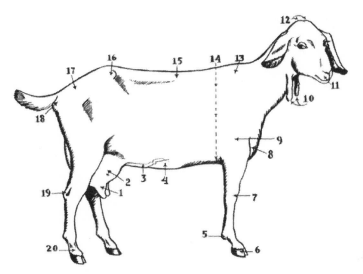

Diagram Showing Parts of a Goat's Body:

1. teats

2. udder

3. milk vein

4. belly

5. claw

6. hoof

7. knee

8. chest

125

9. shoulder

10. wattles

11. muzzle

12. knobs

13. withers

14. heart girth

15. back

16. hip bone

17. rump

18. pin bone

19. hock

20. pastern

Experiments at the University of Missouri have shown that the phenothiazine-salt mixture is quite effective *in controlling* parasites of goats and sheep, provided the animals are comparatively free of the parasites at the time they are put on the mixture. The fall and spring treatment is adequate, provided the grounds are not heavily infested with parasites and the phenothiazine-salt mixture is used continuously.

Another serious condition that you may encounter with a milking doe is udder trouble. This may be caused by injury in the pasture. You should see that there are no objects in the pasture such as pieces of wire or stumps sticking out of the ground, or projections from edges of buildings, or any object in the lot where goats are kept that might injure the udder. Also the entrance to the barn and milking stand should be arranged so as to cause the goats no difficulty. Many injuries to the udder may thus be prevented.

Injury may also be caused by overcrowding the doe's udder with milk either through irregularity in milking, through too heavy grain feeding after freshening, or through failure to remove excess milk if her kids are nursing and not taking her output. Twice a day gentle massage of the udder and hot applications are advised to relieve the congestion, plus milking every two hours for sixteen continuous hours and application of a lubricating ointment. The doe must be kept warm and given plenty of clean, dry bedding, and the treatment repeated at frequent intervals until she has recovered. If the doe does not improve quickly under this treatment it is safest to consult the veterinarian as the condition may be due to infection and if neglected might result in the loss of her ability to produce milk, or even in death, and also might spread to other animals in the herd. When any trouble of this kind occurs it is advisable to discontinue the feeding of grain or other foods that stimulate milk production, to discard the milk from the animal, and to milk her last in the string of milkers.

Scours, or diarrhea, may be corrected usually with a dose of oil followed by boiled milk (half the usual amount in the case of a kid being fed milk) to which, if the case is stubborn, browned flour may be added.

In general, goats respond to the same sort of medication for minor digestive disturbances as is given to human beings— baking soda for indigestion; a soap and water enema for constipation; Epsom salts to cleanse the digestive track of irritating substances which may cause scours. For indigestion or impaction, five heaping tablespoonfuls of Epsom salts in a quart of water are given to an adult goat. Repeat in five hours if no action is obtained and at the same time place a tub of fresh water before the animal and withhold all feed for twenty-four hours. If at any time a goat refuses her grain, this should be considered a danger signal that impaction is developing and immediate steps should be taken to prevent further serious symptoms. The next feeding of grain should be withheld and the hay reduced in amount. Very often this will avert an attack of impaction or indigestion.

Occasionally, goats, particularly if kept for a prolonged time in tie-stalls where the platforms become soaked with urine, will develop small eruptions on the teats and udder. These are stubborn things to clear up and can be spread from one to another by the milker. Washing with a mild disinfectant will help and the application of ointment such as is used for diaper rash in babies is effective.

Abscesses sometimes develop about the mouths or jaws of goats. They usually are not painful and are long in developing to the stage where they become soft enough to lance. They should be watched and when ready should be opened, the pus pressed out, and the wound washed with an antiseptic.

Lice sometimes occur, particularly in the early spring before the goat has shed her heavy winter coat. An application of lard and kerosene—two parts lard, melted, to one part kerosene—well emulsified—will usually dispose of these in the older goats. For the kids and pregnant does a non-poisonous powder, such as is used for dogs, is safer. Your feed dealer will have several brands from which you may choose. What appears to be the best treatment of all is a 5 per cent or 10 per cent powder of DDT rubbed into the hair; this is safe and effective.

Aside from unpredictable problems that may arise at kidding time and which are not frequent, goats given reasonably good care and food will go through life with a clean bill of health—good insurance risks—and live to a ripe old age, barring accident. At present my herd includes a doe twelve years old, two does eleven and one ten. They are sound and healthy and active, have excellent teeth and none has ever been ill. They are still milkers, although giving less milk than in their prime. If you take proper care of your animals you have every right to expect as good results.

A surprisingly large number of goats die from accident, and in most cases these accidents can be avoided. A rope dangling from a hook where a kid can play with it is one way of inviting trouble; or a goat tethered with a thin, cotton rope or in a spot where she can tangle herself if frightened, another. If your goat is tied where you can't readily see her, visit her occasionally to be sure that she is safe. I've known of a goat eating a broom which caused her death, and the moral of that is: put your cleaning equipment in a closet or a room where the goats can't get at it, and keep it there with the door closed securely. Also put your grain some place where the goats can't gorge themselves on it when you are not around. That, too, can bring disaster. A water pail with the handle that swung over the goat's head as she drank and frightened her caused another fatality. It is much safer to use a galvanized tub or to have the handle of the pail removed. Bits of wire, or nails or glass get into the feed with tragic results, especially among kids—although this happens far oftener with cattle than with goats.

Get accustomed to anticipating what may happen and take steps to avoid it, and inspect your goats daily. Chances are that then you will detect any trouble before it becomes serious.

15

Goat Milk and Cream

MILK as it comes from the animal, goat or cow, is referred to as raw milk. Very many people whose animals are tested every six months for TB and Bang's disease have no hesitation about using the raw milk if the animals show a clean bill of health, which is usually the case with goats. These people maintain that pasteurization affects the flavor and the calcium and vitamin content of the milk and they prefer it raw. Others, however, feel safer if the milk has been boiled or pasteurized. In some communities the health regulations require that dairies selling milk commercially must have the milk pasteurized, for pasteurization kills the bacteria that cause TB and undulant fever in humans.

Pasteurization* may be done at home by heating the milk to at least 143°F. and holding it at this temperature for at least 30 minutes, then cooling it rapidly; or by heating it to at least 160°F. and holding it at this temperature for at least 15 seconds, and cooling rapidly. Use a dairy thermometer for this—it must not be done by guesswork and be sure that every drop of the milk receives the heating. To keep the milk pure, even after pasteurization, it must have the same careful handling and refrigeration as in its raw state.

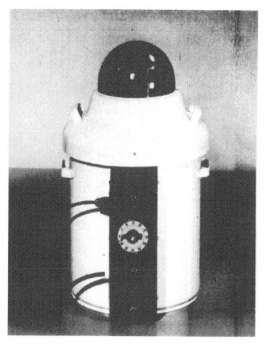

*This is an electric, home-size pasteurizer ideal for small dairies;
it sells for around $40. It makes pasteurizing easy and elimi-
nates the chance of getting TB or Undulant Fever.*

In *Technical Bulletin #46* of the New York Agricultural
Experiment Station the following figures are given on the
comparative food value of Goat Milk, Cow Milk and Human
Milk.

	Fat	Milk Sugar	Per cent Protein combined with Calcium	Salts
Goat Milk	3.80	4.50	3.10	.939
Cow Milk	3.90	4.90	3.20	.901
Human Milk	3.30	6.50	1.50	.313

A similar analysis in the book, "Milk and Milk Products," by Eckles, Combs and Macy gives the following:

	Fat	Lactose	Per cent Protein	Ash	Water
Goat Milk	3.82	4.54	3.21	.55	87.88
Cow Milk	3.80	4.80	3.50	.65	87.25
Human Milk	3.11	7.18	1.19	.21	88.30

From these figures it is notable that while the constituents of goat milk and cow milk do not differ greatly in percentage, human milk shows a lower percentage of protein and a higher percentage of lactose, or milk sugar, than either goat or cow milk. In fact in the Milk and Milk Products table which lists also the analysis of the milk of the sheep, mare, water buffalo, reindeer, camel, sow, bitch, and cat, human milk is lowest in protein and highest in lactose of all the milk analyzed.

The great value which goat milk possesses lies principally in the fact that it forms small, soft curds in the stomach and that the fat globules are small and well emulsified, which makes the milk easily and quickly digested. For this reason it is often advised by physicians for infant feeding, although usually in modified form for the infants, with the addition of malt sugar, or honey, and boiled one minute or pasteurized. Because of its delicacy and easy digestibility it is especially beneficial for invalids or people with low vitality or sensitive digestive systems. Also, in many instances it can be tolerated by people allergic to the protein of cow milk, especially when the allergy results in eczema, hay fever or asthma.

A neighbor of mine occasionally stopped in for a small bottle of goat milk, much as one would stop at a soda fountain. Then one day she explained that she had been using the milk in her nostrils for an irritation of the mucous membrane. She insisted that the milk had cured the irritation. This was too farfetched for my credulity, and I thought of the scripture quotation, "Thy faith hath made thee whole." Who knows? Cleopatra took her milk baths—probably of goat milk— why? If it was just to be clean she could have found plenty of water in the Nile. There are countless cases of people with one ailment or another who give to goat milk credit for their recovery. One trade publication carried an article by a man who put himself on a goat milk diet to cure pyorrhea and claimed that it was successful. Some of these "cures" even though unscientific are not unworthy of consideration when they come from reliable sources. However, goat milk need not be regarded as a nostrum, or a cure-all intended only for the sick or undernourished, and it isn't wisdom to put oneself on a diet of any milk, even goat milk, exclusively. According to scientific authorities, while milk is an excellent food for adults as well as for children, the amount of milk needed for an adult limited to milk alone would be eight to eleven pounds (about four to five and a half quarts) a day, and the protein content is too high and the solid material too concentrated for the average adult (Eckles, Combs and Macy).

Goat milk has its place as a healthful, energy producing food and a delicious beverage for the sick and the well. I know of no milk so refreshing or equal in flavor to a glass of cold, clean, raw goat milk. If you tire of it occasionally as is, try ginger ale with it, fifty-fifty. It is a real thirst quencher on a hot day. Or make iced coffee and use the whole milk in it, not just the cream. Even a gourmet would enjoy it.

The Agricultural College Experiment Station of New Mexico in *Bulletin #154* reports an interesting test regarding the flavor of goat milk as compared with cow milk. A sample of each was given to twelve persons, men and women. No explanation was made and no indication given them that the milk was from animals of different species. It was just milk. They were asked which they preferred. Seven of the twelve chose the goat milk. A similar test was made with fourteen students at State College, New Mexico. Eight preferred the goat milk, four cow milk and two had no preference.

One sometimes meets the comment "but you can't get cream from goat milk!" You can, indeed, although because of the small fat globules and the more complete emulsification it takes longer for cream to rise on goat milk than on cow milk, unless a cream separator is used. With a small separator, however, the goat milk separates just as quickly as the cow milk.

You can make butter from goat milk; also cheese; ice cream from the cream and sherbet from the whole milk; and in the preparation or cooking of any food requiring milk, goat milk functions just as adequately as cow milk. Try cream soups or clam chowder or oyster stew made with goat milk and prove it yourself.

* "The Effect of Pasteurization on some Constituents and Properties of Goat Milk" Haller, Babcock and Ellis, *U. S. Department of Agriculture Technical Bulletin 800*, says:

"The milk was pasteurized by holding it for 30 minutes at a temperature of from 142-147°F., or by bringing it to 160°F. for 15 seconds. The solubility of calcium (lime) and phosphorus was only slightly decreased, to an extent less than the normal variation in composition. The protein was not appreciably affected, but the curd tension was considerably reduced by the 30-minute method and only slightly reduced by the 15-second method. The flavor is said to have been slightly improved and the keeping qualities considerably improved. The phosphates test which is usually applied to cow milk to determine the efficiency of pasteurization could not be applied to goat milk as the phosphate enzyme is destroyed very rapidly. The vitamin C content was reduced about 40 per cent by the 30-minute method and not at all by the 15-second method."

16

Making Butter at Home

AT ONE TIME I visited the owner of a large herd of goats, and as we talked the man who did the milking appeared with a pail of milk—gallons of it—that he poured into a galvanized tub for three or four large dogs to drink. I shrank a little mentally, almost as though the milk had been tossed into my face, for I have a high regard for goat milk as human food and could think of other dishes more suitable for feeding grown dogs. The owner remarked that they had more milk than they could use, and I wondered why they didn't make butter. To be sure it is some trouble, but no more than the making of butter from cow milk.

There are several methods for extracting the cream. Many home buttermakers still cling fondly to the old-fashioned "shallow pan" method. The milk is placed in flat pans and set in a cool place until the cream rises. The cream is then taken off with a "skimmer"—a slightly concave disc with perforations through which the skim milk drains back as the cream is lifted out. The trouble with this is that despite your best efforts there is always danger of dust and bacteria getting into the milk.

There is another method, the "deep setting" method in which the milk while still warm is poured into a "shot-gun" can immersed in cold water (preferably ice water). The cream is skimmed off, or poured off unless the can is equipped with a spigot for drawing off the cream and skim milk separately. This method takes about half as long as the shallow pan method.

The most modern method, however, and by far the best, is the centrifugal separator. With this method the warm milk (which should be 80 to 90° F.) is poured into the separator. This whirls it around and in a jiffy out comes the cream through one spout, the skim milk through another. This is especially desirable for separating goat milk, as goat cream, because of its greater emulsification, rises more slowly than the cream of cow milk, and some goat milk as it ages develops a cheesy or "goaty" flavor which makes the butter unpalatable.

If buttermaking is to be included in your accomplishments, a separator is a good investment. The cost is between $20 and $30 for a small, table model, and it is one of those things that proves its value in the greater efficiency with which it accomplishes your purpose, not from the viewpoint of "Do I get my money back through its use?"

Cornell Extension Bulletin #269, quoting from *Bulletin #116* of the Indiana Agricultural Experiment Station, has a table that gives the figures showing the amount of butterfat retained in skim milk in various methods of separation:

Method	Percentage of Milk Fat
Modern	0.02
Deep-setting	0.17
Shallow pan	0.44
Water dilution	0.68

The "water dilution" method, in which water is added to the milk to aid in creaming, is considered least satisfactory. It means loss of butterfat, water-flavored butter, and diluted, watery skim milk, unsuitable for cheese making or other household use and even for animal feeding.

Installing a separator, however, is no easy job for a woman unless she has a flair for the mechanical. It has many tricky little pieces—set screws, discs, etc., and must be set in place with the guidance of a spirit level, but the instructions for putting it together are simple in man's language, and almost any man can cope with them successfully.

If you purchase a separator have it installed in a cool, clean place and be sure that it is properly balanced and firmly set. Otherwise you will run into difficulty, for the machine is delicately constructed and must be protected against uneven wear on its carefully adjusted parts. Sterilize it each time after use, just as you would any other utensil used in buttermaking. This is important, as stale milk in the separator means fertile soil for bacteria.

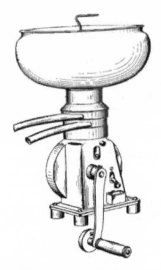

This small separator sells for around $30.

COOLING THE CREAM

After the milk is separated, place the cream immediately in cold water (not in the refrigerator). Water will cool it more rapidly and uniformly than cold air. Mix it occasionally with an up-and-down motion. There is a special "stirring rod" made for this purpose, or you can use an ordinary perforated vegetable ladle with a long handle. When cooled, place the cream in the refrigerator until you are ready to use it.

PREPARING THE CHURN

Small churns for home buttermaking may be secured from dairy supply houses or mail order houses at prices ranging from $2 to $5. If your churn is of glass it needs the same care as your milking equipment—immediate washing after use and sterilizing before the butter is made, followed by rinsing in cold water. A wooden churn should be scalded with boiling water, then chilled with cold water before use. If you make butter only occasionally, fill the churn with hot water at least twenty-four hours before you churn so that the wood will expand (otherwise it may leak) and then be sure that you rinse it with cold water.

For small amounts of butter many people find the electric cake mixer a very satisfactory churn.

PREPARING THE CREAM

A gallon of cream will make two or three pounds of butter and in using goat milk it may be necessary to hold the cream from several milkings in the refrigerator before there is enough to work with. Each lot must be kept separate and none of it should be more than three or four days old. Old cream makes inferior butter that deteriorates rapidly unless pasteurized.

About twelve hours before you plan to churn put all the cream together and mix it thoroughly with your stirring rod to give it uniform thickness.

When you are ready to make the butter warm the cream slowly to 65–75°F. Use a dairy thermometer for this (you can purchase one for about a dollar). Mix the cream frequently with the stirring rod or ladle, and keep it at this temperature until it becomes thick and glassy and tastes a little sour.

Reduce the temperature of the thickened cream rapidly to 52–60°F. in the summer, 58–68°F. for butter made in the cold weather, and hold it at this point for at least two hours.

CHURNING

In pouring the cream into the churn pass it through a strainer so that any lumps will be broken up, and have the churn 1/3 full of cream to prevent overcrowding as the butter expands. Goat milk makes white butter and always needs a few drops of vegetable coloring to give it the shade you like (10 to 20 drops per pound of finished butter).

After the cream and coloring have been placed in the churn turn the handle about ten times, stop and remove the plug or lift the cover of the churn to let the gas escape. Replace the plug, turn the handle about twenty times and again let out the gas. Continue churning until the butter granules are about the size of a pea. Start churning at a speed which will produce the greatest concussion which can be determined by the sound—about 60 revolutions per minute for the common barrel type of churn. Too fast churning makes cream cling to the one end rather than fall from one end of churn to the other as it should. As you become adept at buttermaking the change in the churning sound from a swish to a heavier sound will tell you how you are progressing. In thirty or forty minutes the butter should be formed.

Left. In churning butter cream is heated to 52–60° F. in summer; 58–66° F. in winter, then strained into clean churn.
Right. Churn should be only 1/3 to 1/2 full. Next butter color is added.

WASHING THE BUTTER

Drain off the buttermilk at this point through the strainer to rescue any butter particles in the milk, and pour water of the same temperature as the buttermilk over the granules. Have about as much water as there is buttermilk. Close the churn and turn it a few times rapidly to wash the butter. Draw this water off, and pour about the same amount of fresh water, at the same temperature, into the churn. If the butter is too soft use colder water for this rinsing, if too hard have the water a little warmer. This water when drained off should come pretty clear. It is important that all the milk be washed out otherwise the butter will develop an unpleasant flavor as the milk proteins deteriorate.

Left. Churn is turned at about 60 revolutions a minute. After a few seconds, remove cover and let gas escape. Repeat 2 or 3 times during early stages. Right. Churn until granules are size of wheat grains. Let out buttermilk through strainer.

Left. Wash butter in twice the amount of clean water as there was buttermilk; water should be same temperature as buttermilk. Add 1/2 water to butter in churn, turn four times, drain—then repeat. Right. Salt (3/4 ounce per pound of butter.) Press butter into a thin layer, then fold into pile and press again. Continue until salt has even distribution and butter has good body.

WORKING THE BUTTER

Remove the butter to your "worker" if you have one, or to a wooden bowl or wooden tray which has been rinsed in cold water. Sift good quality table salt, 3/4 ounce for each pound of butter, over the surface and press the butter into a thin layer with a wooden paddle. Fold it over and press it again. Be careful to press, not smear the butter. Smearing makes it like a salve. When it is firm, close-grained and waxy you have finished and can enjoy your toast.

CARE OF EQUIPMENT

Wash all buttermaking equipment thoroughly before putting it away, with hot, soapy water, rinse it thoroughly and store it where the wooden parts won't become bone dry.

17

Making Cheese From Goat Milk

EXCEPT for some methods of making soft or cottage cheese, all cheese is made by coagulating milk with rennet. It is desirable, however, to hasten the coagulation by adding a starter—which is milk previously coagulated or clabbered by souring. Even in making cottage cheese, the best is made by the additional use of "Junket" rennet tablets, which not only hasten the coagulation, but make a more desirable "sweet curd" cottage cheese. For hard cheese—American cheddar, etc.— only a small amount of starter and more rennet are used; this is necessary in order to produce cheese of the desired texture, the kind that develops in flavor as it ages and should be weeks or months old before being consumed.

Cheese may be made from skim milk, whole milk, or from cream, from whey and from buttermilk.

Cheesemaking is a subtle process, for in addition to the lactic acid bacteria which are propagated through the heat and the addition of rennet or a starter, there are other undesirable bacteria in the milk which become active under the heat. These must be kept at the lowest possible minimum. Your strongest weapon against them is cleanliness—the first and most vitally important factor involved in the making of cheese. Animals must be clean and healthy, kept in clean quarters and the milking done in a clean, dust free place. All milking utensils and all equipment used must be sterilized. This includes knives, spoons, the kettle into which the milk is poured, cheesecloth and muslin drain cloth, the thermometer—every item used in the cheese-making.

The second factor is careful observance of directions, especially with respect to temperature control. Hit or miss guess work will not bring good results.

The third and most difficult factor, involved in making cured or ripened cheese, is the conditions under which the cheese is ripened. Different varieties of cheese, of which there are many, require different conditions of temperature and humidity during the curing period. Before you make a specific kind, be sure that you can meet these conditions. A cheese that starts out with every promise of success, carefully and cleanly made, may through variations in temperature and humidity while curing become greasy and rancid and unfit for use. And remember, too, that cured cheese takes time and patience to make. If you're a person who wants results in a jiffy, don't undertake it.

The best place for curing cheese of the hard type is a root cellar, a spring house, a cool, old-fashioned pantry, or the house cellar if it isn't damp. The temperature should be maintained at 50 to 55°F. and the humidity not more than 85 per cent.

In cheesemaking perhaps more than in most fields, experience is truly the best teacher, and with repeated efforts you learn to recognize the appearance and the feel of the batch that holds promise. You will come to recognize and prevent some of the commoner defects such as:

Sour or acid cheese which results from the use of old milk or from too much whey left in the curd before draining. This, when due to the latter condition, can be avoided by raising the cooking temperature, or by cutting the curd into smaller pieces so that the whey drains off more freely.

Bitter flavor, due to bacteria in the milk. This will not occur if milking conditions and handling are sanitary.

Sweet or fruit flavor also may be due to uncleanliness or to improper development of acidity during making.

Coarse texture, caused by insufficient pressure, or pressure at too low temperature.

Cracks caused by improper bandaging or insufficient pressure, can be corrected by dipping cheese into warm water to soften rind and pressing again.

SOFT CHEESES

During the summer months when milking goats are on pasture they are at their best production and you may have surplus milk for making cheese. Most housewives with an extra quart of milk have made soft cheese now and then with good results either from the whole milk or from skim milk after the cream has been separated for coffee or cereal. It is very easy to make and takes only a little time, but soft cheese has keeping quality of only two or three days and too much should not be made at one time. A gallon of milk will make approximately 1 1/2 pounds of cheese.

Cottage Cheese

The skim milk is allowed to sour naturally at a temperature of 75°F. It can be set on the radiator or the back of the kitchen stove and takes about 24 hours to thicken or clabber.

When it is firm and smooth with a little whey on top it is cut into 3/4" cubes and the container placed in another larger container, holding water of the same temperature—75°F. Very gradually the temperature is raised to 100–110°F., not more than 1 or 2 degrees in five minutes, and the contents stirred gently as it heats, to prevent the curd from becoming lumpy. It is held at this temperature for fifteen to thirty minutes. When a small piece pressed between the fingers holds together and shows no milky leakage the curd is transferred into a sack or drain cloth and hung in a cool place to drain. When cool, salt is mixed gently into the curd, about one teaspoonful to one pound of cheese.

Making Starter

You can make starter from fresh whole milk by placing a small amount—about a pint—in a sterilized jar and setting it aside to sour at a temperature of 70–75°F. Put waxed paper over the top of the jar to keep out dust. When soured the milk should be smooth and free from gas holes, with a sour odor and flavor. Remove the top with a sterilized spoon, cover the jar and set it in the refrigerator until needed.

Before using the starter, mix it evenly by transferring it to another sterilized jar and back to the first one.

The following recipe is for cottage cheese made with starter and 1/8 "Junket" rennet tablet combined:

1   gal. skim milk warmed to 75°F.

3/4   cup starter

1/8   "Junket" rennet tablet dissolved in 4 tbsp. cold water

Add starter to milk, then add 1/8 dissolved "Junket" rennet tablet, stirring thoroughly.

Hold milk at 75°F. until smooth, firm curd has formed.

Ladle, without cutting, into sack and drain.

When practically free of whey add salt to taste.

A little cream added to cottage cheese just before serving gives it richness and flavor. It is a very versatile dish and during the warm weather particularly can be made the basis of many delicious salads, with the addition of pimento, chives, chopped radish, sweet peppers or other vegetables. Fruits such as pineapple, orange, grapes or cherries can be worked into delicious, healthful combinations with cottage cheese, or for the children the sweeter fruits like raisins, cooked prunes, peaches or pears have a strong appeal. Experiment with it and find your own favorite combinations.

Best of all, cottage cheese is easily digested and highly nutritious. The Vermont Agricultural Extension Service gives figures showing the relative protein content of cottage cheese as compared with various meats and fish that may surprise you.

One pound of cottage cheese equals in protein:

Beef Rump	1.31 lbs.
Leg of Lamb	1.27 lbs.
Beef Rib Roast	1.55 lbs.
Fowl	1.52 lbs.
Halibut	1.36 lbs.
Salmon	1.51 lbs.
Average	1.36 lbs.

From this average it is evident that the cottage cheese contains one-third more protein than the meat and fish, and when this cheese is made in the home from surplus milk the cost is next to nothing.

Cottage Cheese Omelet

Here are a few simple uses for cottage cheese with fruit:

Cut raisins into pieces and mix with cheese; place on lettuce leaves; top with cherry. Serve with mayonnaise flavored with pineapple juice.

Mold cottage cheese into ball; surround with unstrained cooked cranberries; or mix cranberries into cheese if desired. Serve on lettuce.

The U.S. Department of Agriculture suggests these cottage cheese dishes:

Cottage Cheese Omelet

3	rounded tbsp. cottage cheese
2	eggs
1/4	tsp. salt
1	tbsp. chopped pimentos
2	tbsp. milk
1/8	tsp. soda

Beat yolks and whites of eggs separately. Add to yolks the salt, milk and cheese with which pimentos have been blended. Fold in stiffly beaten whites. Pour into hot frying pan in which 1/2 tbsp. fat has been melted. Cook slowly until egg has set; place in oven to complete cooking; fold in center. Garnish with parsley.

Cottage Cheese and Pimento Roast

2	cupfuls cooked lima beans
3	canned pimentos, chopped
1/4	lb. cottage cheese,
bread crumbs, salt	

Put beans, pimentos and cheese through meat chopper. Mix thoroughly. Add salt. Add bread crumbs until stiff enough to roll. Brown in oven, basting with fat or butter, and water.

Cottage Cheese and Nut Roast

1	cup cottage cheese
1	cup bread crumbs
1	tbsp. butter, (salt, pepper)
1	tbsp. chopped walnuts
2	tbsp. chopped onion

juice of 1/2 lemon

Cook onion in butter and small amount of water until tender. Mix remaining ingredients, moistening with water in which onion has been cooked. Place in shallow baking pan and brown in oven.

Another Soft Cheese, Neufchatel

The French make a soft cheese, Neufchatel, from whole milk, similar in appearance to cottage cheese but, of course, much richer. A delicious cheese of this type requires:

1	gal. sweet, whole milk, tempered to 70°F.
1	"Junket" rennet tablet dissolved in 1/4 cup cold water

Place milk in kettle set in larger kettle containing water of same temperature as the milk, 72°F. The milk is ready for one "Junket" rennet tablet dissolved in 1/4 cup cold water and stirred in thoroughly.

If this is done in the evening, leave undisturbed until morning when the curd should be smooth and firm with very little whey on top. This takes about twelve to fifteen hours.

Ladle the curd into a drain cloth spread over the colander and when fairly dry tie the ends of the cloth and press the curd under a board with a weight on top.

Stir it occasionally to help this whey to drain off.

When dry, add salt to taste.

To ensure a good flavor drain and press the curd in a cool place.

This is delicious. A native Frenchwoman who tried mine immediately wanted to buy some.

Buttermilk Cheese

At the dairy where I went for buttermilk the man said he had never heard of making cheese from it. A neighbor who made butter also had never heard of the cheese. I tried several recipes and got best results from the following:

Heat sour buttermilk slowly to 95°F. Cover and leave undisturbed for about one and a half hours. Then raise temperature very slowly to 140°F. and hold at this temperature until the curd sinks. Drain and salt to taste.

This makes a delicate, soft cheese, fine textured and creamy.

Processed Cheese

This cheese is a little more complicated, but not difficult to make and well worth the extra work.

10	qts. thickly clabbered milk
4	tbsp. butter
3/4	tsp. soda
1 1/2	tsp. salt
2/3	cup sour cream
1/8	cheese color tablet if desired.

Heat milk gradually to 125°F., stirring occasionally.

Ladle into drain sack and hang until dry, mixing curd occasionally to hasten draining.

When dry add 4 tbsp. butter, 3/4 tsp. soda, 1 1/2 tsp. salt, mixing it in gently.

Press down in bowl and set in warm place for two and a

half hours.

Place curd in double boiler, add 2/3 cup sour cream, 1/8 tsp. cheese coloring dissolved in 1/4 cup water and heat until liquid.

Pour into jars and seal.

Mysost

Every time I made cheese and saw the clear, pale greenish whey disappearing down the drain I felt guilty. I knew that it had food value and it seemed unpardonable to waste any. I had no pig and no chickens, but put out a pan for Chester and Mabel, the ducks. They washed their bills in it, but as food it had no interest for them. I set out a sample for the cat. She took a few sips and walked away. Some of the older goats drank it but next day had a tendency toward scours. As the young kids were on a strictly whole milk diet it wasn't safe to give them any.

I read about whey and found that it contains most of the lactose or sugar of the milk, minerals and albumin. And I learned that among Scandinavian people this whey is boiled down and made into primost or mysost. So I tried it.

Strain the whey and boil it down rapidly, stirring almost constantly. Skim off the albumin that rises to the top, and when the whey is reduced to about one-quarter the original amount put this albumin back and stir it in thoroughly. Continue boiling until it becomes thick. Pour quickly into a wooden bowl and stir it until cool to prevent sugar crystals from forming.

The boiling down process is a lengthy one and the almost constant stirring necessary to prevent scorching becomes a bit tedious, but the fruit of your effort is an attractive spread about the color of maple sugar, sweet and bland that some people find delicious.

HARD CHEESES

From time to time I looked over recipes for cured or ripened cheese. The array of figures and the hoops and molds mentioned frightened me off. I got the impression that hard cheese-making was involved and difficult. Then a friend told me that he had a simple recipe given him by a Frenchman and he would show me how the cheese was made.

The recipe *was* simple and easy to follow, but like the old lady who marked her pies "TM"—" 'tis Mince" and " 't'aint Mince"—he couldn't tell with any sureness which of his cheeses were good and which were not good, and they all had quite a coating of colorful mold, which meant waste. The sample I had was a " 'tis good" and I decided to try the recipe.

Coffee cans such as he used for molds were hard to find as coffee was being packed in jars and paper bags, but finally I located two bright, new ones and punctured the bottoms with holes to allow the whey to drain off. Then I made little wooden discs, a shade smaller than the circumference of the cans, called "followers" in the cheese business.

The cheese looked right and the curd was dipped into the cans which were lined with cheesecloth, the little wooden followers placed on top, and for weight a quart bottle of water set on top of each cheese. During the night I heard a crash in the kitchen and rushed out to stalk the burglar. I found that the pressure of the curd had pushed the bottles off the cheese, spilling the water. The resilience of that curd astonished me. Flashlight in hand, I hurried out to the stone wall and groped about for two smooth, round stones which I scrubbed and placed on the cheese for weights. Next day when the cheese was removed from the molds the edges had to be trimmed and the top surface smoothed off where the folds of the cheesecloth had left ridges—more waste.

My friend cured his cheese in a root cellar. I had none and decided that the stone garage would do, but in a few days mold developed. This I wiped off with warm salt water and transferred the cheeses to the milk room. A nice yellow rind began to form. Then there came a week of stifling hot weather. The cheeses sweated, grew hard and rancid. Much discouraged I tossed one out to my neighbor's cat. She struggled with it, holding it down with her paw, but even her sharp teeth could make no impression on the tough rind and she gave it up. I gathered up all the cheeses, about a half dozen, concluded that with cured cheese I was a failure, and put them in the garbage can. Later I learned that the well is a very good place for curing cheese made during hot weather.

Then I came upon the Hansen chart for making hard cheese; it looked so simple that I tried again. Over a period of several weeks I made two cheeses a week. When they were cured a neighbor bought one at $1.25 a pound, and within a half-hour brought in a friend who wanted one to take back to the city. Another cheese I kept in an electric refrigerator for a year. No mold developed and it held its fine aroma and flavor. It grew hard enough to grate, and yet could be sliced very thin.

I called these cheeses a great success.

Hansen's Hard Cheese *

163

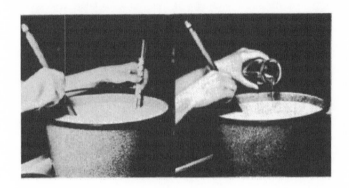

Left. Warm the Milk to 86° F.

Use an enameled or tinned pail and heat 8 quarts (2 gallons) sweet whole milk to 86° F. You may use either cow's or goat's milk, with equally good results. If yellow cheese is desired, dissolve an eighth of Cheese Color Tablet in a tablespoon of water and stir into milk.

Right. Add Cheese Rennet

Then add 1/4 of a Cheese Rennet Tablet (or 2 1/2 "Junket" Rennet Tablets) dissolved in 1/2 cup cold water. Mix thoroughly. Set in a pan of warm water (85 to 90° F.)

* Directions given by permission of Chr. Hansen's Laboratory.

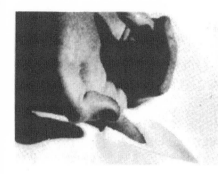

Left. Let Set Until "Clean Break"

Let stand until a firm curd forms, about 30 minutes. Test the firmness of curd with your finger. Put your finger into the curd at an angle and lift it. If the curd breaks clean over the finger it is ready to cut. (See diagram *below*.)

Right. Warm Slowly to 90–100° F.

Heat the water in the outside pan slowly—allow 1/2 to 3/4 hour to raise temperature to 90–100° F. Stir the curd with your hand very gently at the beginning, so as not to get too many very small pieces of curd. During the entire time of heating, stir frequently enough to keep the temperature even throughout—and to keep the pieces of curd from sticking. Cut with your knife any pieces of curd that are very large; they should all be as uniform as possible.

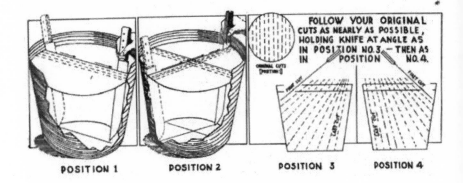

POSITION 1   POSITION 2   POSITION 3   POSITION 4

Cut 2 Ways Vertically—Then 2 Ways at an Angle.

Use a long butcher knife or pancake turner—long enough so that the blade will go to the bottom of the pail without the handle dipping into the curd. Cut into squares of about 3/8″ (Positions 1 and 2). Use your knife at an angle—(Position 3)—starting about 1–1 1/2″ from side of pail; with angular cuts, slice curd into pieces about 1/2–1″ thick; begin at top, and make each cut about 1/2–1″ lower. Turn pail and draw similar angular cuts from other side (Position 4).

Left. Pour Curd into Cheese Cloth to Form Round Ball.

When curd is firm enough so it has little tendency to stick together, pour into a cloth about 2 to 3 feet square and form into a ball. Hang it up until all the free whey has dripped off—2 to 3 hours. *Right.* Dress the Cheese

Then remove the cloth from the sides of the ball, and place the ball on a cheese cloth folded over 3 or 4 times. Fold a long cloth, shaped like a dish towel, into a bandage about 3 inches wide and wrap tightly around the ball of curd. Pin in place. With your hands, press cheese down and make the surface of the top smooth by crumbling with your fingers. There should be no cracks extending into the center of the cheese.

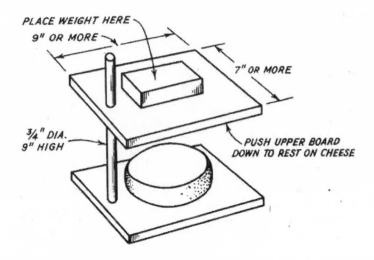

PLACE WEIGHT HERE
9" OR MORE
7" OR MORE
3/4" DIA.
9" HIGH
PUSH UPPER BOARD
DOWN TO REST ON CHEESE

Then Press the Cheese

Lay a piece of wet cloth over the top of the cheese; place a flat plate over the cloth and a weight about equal to a flatiron or a brick. You might find that the weight is likely to fall over to one side, giving the cheese an odd shape; in that case, make a simple cheese press from two boards and a round stick, as illustrated. Your round loaf of cheese should not be more than 6" across; otherwise it will dry out too much. At night turn cheese and place the weight on top of it again. Let stand until morning.

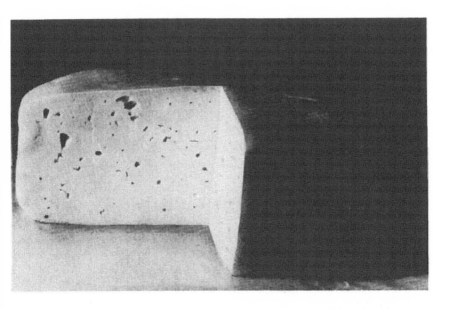

Store in Cool Place, Salt and Rub

Remove the cloth and bandage and place on a board, if possible in a cool but frost-free place, like the cellar. Turn once or twice a day until a rind is formed. This probably will take three days. Then rub a tablespoonful of salt into the cheese two days in succession. After this rub thoroughly 1 or 2 days with a very small amount of butter; rub and turn the cheese each day until the rind is very firm. After a week or two it will not be necessary to rub so frequently. Two or three times a week will keep it from getting dry and prevents mold from developing.

The cheese can be sold after 3 weeks but will be better after 4—6 weeks' curing at 50—55° F., if stored under proper conditions. A good clean cellar is usually the best place; it should not be so moist that cheese will mold, but on the other hand, not so dry that rind will crack.

Wisconsin Brick Cheese

Another similar appetizing cured cheese is Wisconsin Brick Cheese, made as follows:

3	gals. sweet, whole milk
1/3	Rennet Tablet dissolved in 1/3 cup cold water

Heat milk gradually to 86°F. Remove from heat and add 1/3 rennet tablet dissolved in 1/3 cup cold water, stirring thoroughly. Let stand about a half hour, until curd shows a clean break. Cut into cubes 3/8 to 1/2″ in size.

Heat slowly to 98°F., stirring while heating. Remove from heat and stir with gentle, folding motion for thirty minutes.

Pour off most of whey and work 2 tbsps. salt gently into curd. Place in mold and press for six hours; turn cheese and press for twelve hours.

Rub with salt and store in moderately cool place. In two

days rub again with salt.

Turn daily for two to three weeks when it should be ready for use. If mold develops remove with lukewarm salt water.

The mold for this cheese should be of wood, rectangular in shape, like a bottomless box, with holes bored at two-inch intervals to permit whey to escape, and a follower fitted snugly inside and resting upon the curd and weighted with a brick. I bandaged mine in the same manner as the cheese made from the Hansen directions with entirely satisfactory results, although the shape was round, not rectangular.

As I put away the cheesemaking equipment I noted with amusement that except for a dairy thermometer and ply-board for the press, the entire equipment went back onto the pantry shelves. It consisted of:

1 large kettle to serve as a vat into which the milk is placed. This must be of tinware or enamel.

1 larger kettle into which the first kettle is set for heating the milk.

1 dipper with holes for dipping out the curd. Desirable but not essential.

1 tablespoon, 1 teaspoon, 1 large spoon (preferably wooden).

1 long-bladed knife or spatula.

1 good-sized sugar or salt sack or a square yard of unbleached muslin or cotton cloth for draining the curd.

1 cup.

1 colander or strainer.

1 dairy thermometer (This I had to purchase at $1.50).

Smooth boards for making press.

A Few Precautions

For good results with cheesemaking there are a few precautions to be kept always in mind.

Be sure that the milk from which the cheese is made is clean and wholesome and of good flavor. Don't use old milk.

Have all utensils sterilized.

Follow directions carefully.

Be watchful of temperatures; use your thermometer.

Increase heat gradually.

Stir the curd gently.

Bandage carefully and smoothly, otherwise your cheese may crack.

Use sufficient pressure to expel the whey.

18

What to Do With Manure

DAILY cleaning of the barn or goat shed is a never ending chore and it means an endless supply of manure. If you have just a few goats the disposition of the manure is no problem. It makes one of the finest fertilizers for the vegetable and flower gardens and for those bare spots here and there where grass is so reluctant to grow. If there is more manure than you need, the neighbors will be glad to have the extra, particularly when they realize that it is not messy to have on their grounds, and practically odorless. One of my neighbors sent his man for a load of manure and as he piled it onto the truck the man remarked several times in a most puzzled tone, "There's no smell to it." Another neighbor sent for some which he placed in a fifty-gallon barrel with a spigot at the bottom. He added water and from time to time this was drawn off through the hose for watering his garden. You never saw finer garden vegetables.

If the manure is to be stored for later use it should be wheeled some distance from the barn and placed preferably in a covered pit to protect it from rains and from heating and fermentation. If it is to be stacked in mounds the sides should be straight and banked with boards to prevent slipping and washing down and the top depressed toward the center. The mounds should be covered, but moistened occasionally to prevent drying out.

Where there are many goats and the amount of manure is appreciable, it is not difficult to find a gardener or a florist who will buy it provided it is free of hay seeds, and these seeds can be killed by composting the manure. Prior to the war, sheep and goat manure sold at $2 a hundred-pound sack, and with the universal interest in gardening, properly prepared goat manure might well repay the goat owner for the little care and trouble he must take in making it marketable.

Even without special care goat manure is salable, although the, price received for manure in open piles is considerably less, usually about the same price as cow manure.

Goats kept in tie-stalls require no bedding and very little hay gets into the manure in the gutters, but much of the value of the manure is in the urine which the animals void and which in many cases drains off into the cesspool or into the open ground. It might be feasible to pipe this drain directly into the pit in which the manure is dumped or into a sunken container from which it can be drawn off for use in fertilizing. Absorbent material such as sawdust, peat moss or sugar-cane litter, placed in the gutters will retain much of the urine.

Super-phosphate under the absorbent material will help to eliminate odors and increase the value of the manure.

19

Goats as a Business

MORE or less frequently one meets the question, "Is there money in it?" It is difficult to give an answer that the questioner will understand, but it would seem that if your chief purpose in having goats is to make money you would do better with less effort in some other field. There are people who find goats profitable, modestly so, either in combination with some other activity such as chicken raising, or as a full-time venture, but they are people who, first of all, have goats because they love them. In addition to the return in dollars and cents they value the less tangible compensation such as comes, for example, in an afternoon in the woods with the herd, and the feeling of quiet peace it brings.

If you think of going into goat raising as a business be very sure that you have the temperament for the work. It requires, above all else, limitless, untiring patience. Plenty of people have started goat raising only to give up in a short time. They will tell you that the work is too hard; the goats require too much care; it's too confining. All this is true, but if you like it you can omit the "too." Like a physician you are on call twenty-four hours of the day seven days of the week. Goats are naturally exceptionally healthy animals, but it is your care and watchfulness that must keep them healthy. The routine work goes on winter and summer, in good weather and bad, and it must be carried through on schedule or you will run into trouble. During the kidding season it is often necessary to spend the entire night at the barn, and it may be a very cold night. Next day you can't rest and make up the lost sleep, but must carry on as usual.

How many milkers are needed for a family to make a living?
One successful family dairy has 25—plus a retail route.

If members of the family can share the work it makes the going easier, but if outsiders must be employed you still, as owner, must bear the care and worry and keep the ever-watchful eye, for to secure a worker who will have the same interest in your herd as you have is practically impossible—too much to ask of fate. Even if you are worth a million you can't necessarily get the right sort of person to take over. In fact at one time a millionaire goat owner told me he was disposing of his herd of 300 or more because he could find no one to take proper care of them. When my herd was small I boarded them Specifications

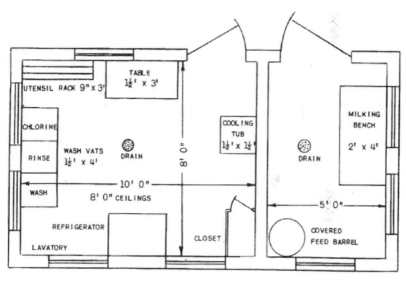

Plans for a "Grade A" Goat Dairy Milk House.

All floors of smooth concrete slope to drains; rounded corners 6 inches about floor level. Walls and ceilings may be painted plywood. All openings screened with 16-mesh wire.

Doors self-closing to open outward. Running water must be piped to the wash vats. Lavatory may consist of wash basin and paper towels. Drains with bell traps; piped 50 feet from building. Steel table. Gasoline or gas heater for heating water, or laundry stove. Tub with ice water for cooling to 50° F. If refrigerator is in satisfactory condition, it may be kept in owner's house.

Utensils

Covered milk buckets—three-quarter top. Metal strainer with cotton pad—no cloth. One valve bottle filler—no pouring. Mechanical hand capper.

Caps purchased in tubes and kept in a clean, dry place. Name of producer and contents printed on cap.

for a few months with a man who considered his herdsman excellent. One day I stopped in at feeding time. My two six-months-old kids were together in a box-stall, which was nice for companionship, but they had one feed box between them and the more aggressive kid got the food which was dumped into the box on top of the stale, left-over bits and a few sprinklings of manure from the kids' hoofs. These are the conditions that the watchful goat owner would guard against.

If you are primarily interested in dairying, be sure that you are accessible to customers, both for their sake and for your own, for your location will do much to advertise your dairy, and though goat milk may be as desirable as that proverbially superior mousetrap, customers won't blaze a trail to your dairy to obtain it. Acquaint yourself fully with the state and local requirements for selling milk. Recognize that selling goat milk is a job that requires constant effort. It isn't like the sale of cow milk. Every family uses cow milk and when a new family comes into a neighborhood it is only a question of which milkman gets there first—the customer is waiting. With goat milk you will find that someone's baby will need the milk and then as the child progresses the mother will one day tell you "I'm going to put him on cow milk now." Your customer is gone and you must find another to take his place. Some days you won't have enough milk to supply the calls and you will begin to wonder if you should expand, then a slump will come and you will think of the mounting feed bills and perhaps sell off some of your stock only to regret it later. If you raise your own hay and grain this is a lesser worry, but even so, you don't like to lose customers.

Another important matter to keep in mind if you are dairying is a steady flow of milk. Many customers are lost because the dairy has to post a sign or notify its customers some time in the late fall or winter months—"No milk available until January." For customers allergic to cow milk or babies on a goat milk diet this is serious, and it behooves you to arrange your breeding schedule so as to avoid so far as possible this shortage. Make a list or chart of your does and plan their breeding as follows:

As early as possible, in August or September, breed the yearlings and does whose lactation is slowing down, provided those does have not freshened too recently. To maintain their good health and vigor they should not be expected to kid more than once a year.

The main advantage of a milking machine is in speeding up the milking—and it's easier to buy a milking machine than find a good milker.

In October and November breed the next group, saving for December, January and February breeding your best milkers—those with longest lactation period.

In this way you will have does freshening in January and February, March and April, May, June and July. Presumably some of your does, even though pregnant, will continue to milk for at least three months after they are bred and the late fresheners will carry you through the winter months until the first group freshens. Although the breeding season extends into March it is a little risky to hold any does so late as you have less chance to repeat the service in case it is not effective.

Be very sure that you supervise this breeding schedule yourself. During October one season it was necessary for me to be away for a week and I gave instructions that one doe who had freshened in July should not be bred. She was a Nubian with distinct individual markings and there should have been no misunderstanding, but on my return I found that she was the only doe that had been bred. At kidding time she died. Recently a customer who had purchased a young doe wrote that she was disappointed in the production of Daisy. It astonished me that Daisy had been bred at just six months old, and I learned that the owner was away when Daisy came in heat and the hired man had bred her.

The breeding end of the goat business seems to be the more

popular. For one thing a goat breeder can locate on cheaper land, provided he is accessible to a railroad station for shipping stock. He has less routine milking and kid feeding to do as he can leave the kids to suckle from their mothers. He doesn't worry about the loss of milk customers or hustle about to find new ones, and any excess milk he can convert into butter or cheese for his own use. To be sure he must find customers for his stock, but that isn't difficult if he has good animals and advertises in the right publications.

During the war, which prevented the importation of foreign cheeses, a very active interest developed in the making of cheese from goat milk. In some cases a herd is maintained to provide milk and, in addition, milk from dairies is purchased. A business of this sort calls for quite some investment in cheesemaking equipment and the employment of skilled workers to make the cheese. If you are located near such a plant you might find it profitable to arrange with them to take over your surplus milk, provided you can meet their requirements.

On the Pacific Coast, at Soledad, California, the Meyenberg Milk Products Company, originators of the evaporation process for cow milk, have a plant for the evaporation and canning of goat milk. This sort of venture also requires heavy investment and full knowledge of how it is done.

Tie stalls in a commercial dairy.

There are also some people who have gone into the cosmetic field, making creams and lotions from goat milk and whey. If you have a knowledge of chemistry this field might bear looking into, as very little has been done in it thus far.

Whatever branch of the goat business you undertake be sure that your barn, however simple, is clean and attractive, and your animals also. Have your equipment as complete as you can afford so that you won't suffer the nervous strain and the extra work that comes with makeshifts.

Appendix

Milk Goat Registry Associations:

The American Milk Goat Record Association,

Sherborn, Massachusetts.

The American Goat Society, Inc.,

Columbia, Missouri.

Milk Goat Magazines:

American Dairy Goat News,

Richmond (19), Virginia.

Better Goatkeeping,

Ipswich, Massachusetts.

Dairy Goat Journal,

Columbia, Missouri.

The Goat World,

Portland (7), Oregon.

Made in the USA
Middletown, DE
26 December 2018